Exploring Southern Utah's Land of Color

BY Arthur F. Bruhn REVISED AND UPDATED BY Nicky Leach

Contents

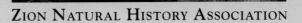

ZION NATURAL HISTORY ASSOCIATION

D1403924

Copyright 1993 by Zion Natural History Association, Zion National Park, Springdale, Utah 84767; (801) 772-3264

This book, or parts thereof, may not be reproduced in any form without permission.

Coordinated by Jamie Gentry
Edited by Edna Gregerson
Photography by Clint Crawley
Illustrations by Fred Harrison
Design by Rebecca Livermore
Area map by Rebecca Livermore

Printed in the United States of America by Paragon Press

ISBN No. 0-915630-32-X
Library of Congress
Catalog No. 93-060269

First printing of revised edition, 1993

Cover photograph: Navajo sandstone, Snow Canyon State Park

Inside cover: Grosvenor Arch

Back cover: The top of the Great White Throne in afternoon shadow, Zion National Park

Acknowledgments

We would like to thank the following people and organizations for their help in updating Arthur Bruhn's original book:

The Bruhn family, especially Lorna Bruhn and Ross Hurst; J.L. Crawford, author/historian; Dr. Karl Brooks, mayor of St. George and son of Mormon historian/author Juanita Brooks; Tim Manns, former chief interpreter, Zion National Park; Tim Duck, biologist, BLM; Audrey Shumway, head librarian, Dixie College; Dr. Wes Larsen, author/historian; Bart Anderson, southern Utah historian and Utah state medical examiner investigator; Gary L. Tom, education director, Paiute Indian Tribe of Southern Utah; Wilson Hunter and Max King, NPS interpretors, Canyon de Chelly National Monument; Floyd Fox, Washington County Chamber of Commerce; Utah Travel Council; Ron Thompson and the staff of the Washington County Water Conservancy District; and the staff of Zion Natural History Association.

Bibliography

Barnes, F.A., *Utah Canyon Country* (Salt Lake City, UT: Utah Geographic Series, Inc., 1986)

Brooks, Juanita, *The Mountain Meadows Massacre* (Norman, OK: University of Oklahoma Press, 1950)

Brooks, Juanita, *Quicksand and Cactus, A Memoir of the Southern Mormon Frontier* (Salt Lake City: Howe Brothers Publishers, 1982)

Crawford, J.L., *Zion National Park, Towers of Stone* (Springdale, UT: Zion Natural History Association, 1988)

Crawford, J.L., *A Zion Album: A Nostalgic History of Zion Canyon* (Springdale, UT: Zion Natural History Association, 1986)

Fowler, Don D., Fowler, Catherine S., & Euler, Robert C., *John Wesley Powell and the Anthropology of the Canyon Country*, Geological Survey Professional Paper 670 (first published Washington, D.C.: United States Government Printing Office, 1969; reprinted by Grand Canyon Natural History Association, AZ: 1977, 1981)

Hamilton, Wayne L., *The Sculpturing of Zion* (Springdale, Utah: Zion Natural History Association, 1984)

Larson, Andrew Karl, *I Was Called to Dixie. The Virgin River Basin: Unique Experiences in Mormon Pioneering*, (St. George, Utah: Andrew Karl Larson, Publisher, 1961)

Lavender, David, *Pipe Spring and the Arizona Strip* (Springdale, UT: Zion Natural History Association, 1984)

Leach, Nicky, *The Guide to National Parks of the Southwest* (Tucson, AZ: Southwest Parks and Monuments Association, 1992)

Markoff, Dena, *An Outstanding Wonder* (Springdale, UT: Zion Natural History Association, 1978)

McPherson, Robert S., *The Northern Navajo Frontier: 1860-1900* (Albuquerque, NM: University of New Mexico Press, 1988)

Netoff, Dennis; Ladd, Gary; Lamb, Susan; Wood, Charles W.; & Holland, James S., *The Lake Powell*

Boater's Guide (Glen Canyon, AZ: Glen Canyon Natural History Association & Grand Canyon Natural History Association, 1989)

Palmer, William, *Why the North Star Stands Still* (Springdale, UT: Zion Natural History Association, 1991)

Rider, Roland (as told to Deidre Murray Paulsen), *The Rollaway Saloon: Cowboy Tales of the Arizona Strip* (Logan, UT: Utah State University Press, 1985)

Smart, William B., *Old Utah Trails* (Salt Lake City, UT: Utah Geographic Series, Inc., 1988)

Weir, Bill, *Utah Handbook* (Chico, CA: Moon Publications, 1989)

Welsh, Dr. Stanley L, *Wildflowers of Zion National Park* (Springdale, UT: Zion Natural History Association, 1991)

Woodbury, Angus M., *A History of Southern Utah and its National Parks* (Salt Lake City, UT: Utah State Historical Society, 1944, 1950 (revised edition))

Foreword

Arthur F. Bruhn was born in Parowan, Iron County, Utah, on September 30, 1916, the son of Peter Frederick and Eleanor Guymon Bruhn. He grew up in Panguitch, Utah, and graduated from high school there. He attended the University of Utah, from 1935 until 1938, then went on to Brigham Young University, from which he graduated in 1940. He married Lorna Chamberlain in June 1939. The couple had four children: Elizabeth, Kay, Marilyn, and Michael.

Arthur Bruhn began his teaching career as principal of Cannonville Elementary School in Garfield County, Utah, then taught science at Cedar City Junior High School and Parowan High School. Mr. Bruhn was an instructor in the Geneva Steel Company training division between 1944 and 1945, after which he returned to BYU to earn his master's degree in zoology. From 1946 to 1953, he taught in the Dixie College biology department in St. George, Utah. He obtained his Ph.D. from the University of Utah the following year and became president of Dixie College.

As a member of the Utah State Park and Recreation Commission, Arthur Bruhn was instrumental in Southern Utah's Snow Canyon being designated a state park. Before becoming president of Dixie College, he worked for 10 years as a seasonal National Park Service ranger at Zion National Park and Cedar Breaks National Monument.

Mr. Bruhn was a splendid teacher, always challenging his students to reach their full potential. He was an author, musician, poet, scientist, historian, naturalist, photographer, and a great friend to many people.

Mt. Abraham in afternoon light,
Zion National Park

Introduction

What is southern Utah's Land of Color? For the purposes of this book, we have chosen to highlight a particularly scenic area of southern Utah stretching from Capitol Reef National Park in the northeast to Newcastle in the northwest, and Glen Canyon National Recreation Area in the southeast to Gunlock Reservoir State Park in the southwest. Three geographical provinces—the Colorado Plateau, the Great Basin, and the Mojave Desert—join in this region, a circumstance that has been instrumental in creating southern Utah's multicolored rocks, convoluted canyons, and remarkable rock formations.

Although it is hard to believe today, this area of the Southwest was still relatively unknown to most Americans until better roads, cars, and facilities began to attract visitors to the region during the postwar period. In addition, in the fifties and sixties, the damming of western rivers like the Colorado brought reliable water to this parched region, starting an unprecedented real estate boom. A second migration to the West began—just over a century after the first pioneers settled here.

The first edition of *Southern Utah's Land of Color* was written in 1952 by Arthur Bruhn, a southern Utah native and prominent St. George resident; it was updated a decade later, shortly before his death. Mr. Bruhn—something of a Renaissance Man when it came to his home state—wished to familiarize visitors with a part of the country that, until then, had remained a mystery to most outsiders. To understand this Land of Color requires some knowledge of the geology and natural and human history that have given southern Utah its special character. His ancestors may have been too busy trying to wrest a living from the land to spend much time extolling its many virtues, but Mr. Bruhn's well-informed homage to the place of his birth quickly corrected this imbalance. His text remains today a fascinating look at a unique place.

In the 30 years since the second edition of the book, some things in southern Utah have hardly changed, while other changes are increasingly affecting the economic direction of the state. But the citizens of

Utah's Dixie are nothing if not adaptable—after the heroic struggles of their pioneer ancestors how could they be anything else—and a new, diversified economy combining agriculture, ranching, tourism, development of real estate and services, and industry is gradually emerging. This third, updated edition of the book reflects many of the transformations taking place here and attempts to place them in context.

The natural resources of the region have attracted people here for thousands of years, but development began in earnest as the land was settled during the mid-1800s. Early in the 20th century, it became clear that overuse was destroying much of southern Utah's natural resources. As a result, many acres of southern Utah's Land of Color have been set aside as national forests, state parks, national parks, and national recreation areas, with each area afforded different degrees of protection and usage according to designation. Today, the public agencies of the National Park Service, the Bureau of Land Management, the U.S. Forest Service, the Bureau of Reclamation, and the Utah State Parks and Recreation Department are responsible for working with the citizens of southern Utah to conserve (and also preserve) the resources that make it unique.

However, as land development continues to put pressure on delicate ecosystems and we understand more about the contribution of wilderness in maintaining nature's balance, it has become increasingly clear that even greater protection is sometimes necessary for particular ecosystems to survive. The Wilderness Act of the 1960s, which paved the way for southern Utah's three wilderness areas, and the Endangered Species Act of the 1970s, which now protects an important subpopulation of Mojave desert tortoise in the Beaver Dam and St. George areas, have begun to change land use patterns in this traditionally agricultural and ranching region.

As more and more retirees and tourists come to southern Utah to take advantage of its clean air, peaceful lifestyle, and myriad recreational opportunities, farming, ranching, and mining of minerals have ceased to be the region's primary occupations. Light industry is increasingly important to the local economy, as are real estate development and the construction of recreational facilities. In fact, activities, such as golfing, bicycling, boating, fishing, hiking, birding, photography, river rafting, skiing, to name but a few, are making southern Utah one of the prime travel destinations in the nation. Fortunately, southern Utah seems to be making the transition gracefully, and perhaps we can look to this part of the state's pioneer history for an explanation. The cooperation that allowed the pioneers to find solutions to problems in the past is again proving useful today as competing interests clamor for a voice in the future of one of America's most resource-rich regions.

Although it is tempting to plan your visit to southern Utah around its more familiar sights, it would be a pity just to stop there. This book is designed to get you off the beaten track, exploring the Scenic Byways and Scenic Backroads that offer a behind-the-scenes look at this area. We recommend that you read the first three sections of the book to gain an important overview of the geology, human history, and wildlife of the region. A fourth section provides guidelines on successfully photographing this photogenic landscape. The heart of the book is an alphabetical listing of the wonderful cities, towns, hamlets, and ghost towns found throughout southern Utah, together with their histories. Many sidebars provide additional information about particular events and individuals who have contributed to a town's history, discussions of unique geological features worth a side trip, as well as tips on taking photographs in several national parks. It is our hope that this book will be a constant companion for your exploration of southern Utah's Land of Color.

Nicky Leach
October 1992

An Historic Overview of Southern Utah

The following chapter serves as an introduction to the vibrant history of southern Utah. Included are sections on the region's American Indian inhabitants, the first European explorations by the Spanish in the 18th century, subsequent travels through Utah by explorers, mountain men, and traders in the early 1800s, Mormon colonization from the mid-1800s on, ending with a look at southern Utah today.

We hope this account will give readers an understanding of the events that have given this part of Utah its particular personality. Although there are several common threads that make up the rich fabric of southern Utah's history, each community has its own unique story. It is our intention to pay tribute to the many fine people who have made their homes here, and to bring to light the qualities that make each of the settlements in southern Utah's Land of Color special.

SOUTHERN UTAH'S NATIVE POPULATIONS

American Indians have used southern Utah and the surrounding areas of the Southwest for thousands of years, although few signs remain of their passage. At least 9,000 years ago, when the climate was more moist and the land more verdant, small groups of nomadic people belonging to the Desert Archaic culture moved around here, gathering seasonal wild foods and hunting small game. They did not build any permanent structures, but we know they passed through because animal remains and stone tools are found from time to time.

Then, around the time of Christ, agriculture reached the Southwest, probably as a consequence of contact between North American natives and Mesoamericans. Cultivation of corn, and later squash and beans, ensured a reliable food supply and made it feasible to stay in one place. This was the beginning of what we know as the Anasazi culture, after the Navajo word *Anasazi*, generally translated as the "Ancient Ones" or "Enemy Ancestors." From simple beginnings, over a period of approximately 1,000 years, the Anasazi culture grew to be the most successful and widespread civilization in the Southwest.

Archeologists generally divide the development of the Anasazi culture into two broad categories (Basketmaker and Pueblo), and then cite subcategories within each one (Basketmaker I, II, and III and Pueblo I, II, and III). Although few scientific studies have been conducted in southern Utah, those that have offer sufficient data for archeologists to correlate the ruins and artifacts found here with both Basketmaker and Pueblo Anasazi.

Evidence suggests that, by A.D. 300, groups of Basketmaker Anasazi were established in semi-subterranean pithouses, practicing dryland farming in gardens, and supplementing their diet by hunting and gathering. It had been thought that

experimentation with crop cultivation and shelter construction continued over a long period, but recent evidence suggests that cultivation was adopted and became widespread very quickly, perhaps indicating the Anasazi were in contact with people who taught them these skills.

Although they made very primitive pots, the early Anasazi favored tightly woven baskets in their day-to-day activities, leading archeologists to call them Basketmakers. Corn was placed in baskets made from the fibers of native plants like yucca and apocynum. Plant fibers were also used in the fabrication of square-toed sandals, string, and rope, and they provided the base for fur robes. Even water could be transported and stored in baskets that were waterproofed with pitch from the piñon tree. Human hair proved useful, too, in weaving and string making.

The Anasazi began to develop storage areas made of slab-lined pits covered with poles, brush,

Anasazi pottery shards

cedar bark and mud to keep their crops from spoiling in the desert heat and from being eaten by rodents. Eventually, storage cists also doubled as graves for the dead. The bodies were flexed with the knees drawn up beneath the chin, and the faces were covered with an inverted basket. Apparently the Anasazi wished their dead to be well prepared for whatever lay ahead, for various tools and implements were often placed near the bodies, and the deceased were equipped with sandals. Sometimes, the bodies would be wrapped in blankets.

FOOD AND TOOLS

In addition to their crops of corn and squash, the Basketmakers ate roots, grass seeds, bulbs, sunflower seeds, piñon nuts, chokecherries, berries, and yucca and cactus fruits. Corn and seeds were ground into a meal between two stones, known as a *mano* and *metate* (these implements were a basic part of Anasazi life and have been found at numerous archeological sites). Birds and small animals were also integral to the diet, and the bones of rabbits, badgers, prairie dogs, and field mice are often present in Anasazi sites. There is evidence also that the Anasazi hunted larger animals such as bison, mammoths, camels, moun-

tain lions, deer, and mountain sheep, eating the meat and using the hides to prepare clothing or to make bags. Bird feathers were prized as decoration. Tools were chiseled from hard stone, such as obsidian, and digging sticks made of hardwood were used for planting crops. Stone awls allowed the Anasazi to cut, scrape, and sew animal hides. In time, contact between Anasazi groups led to the introduction of a spear thrower known as the *atlatl*, which made hunting easier.

PREHISTORIC ARTISTRY

Although hunting and gathering remained integral to Basketmaker life—particularly in southern Utah—reliable crops and the beginnings of communal living allowed the people to experiment with handicrafts. They decorated their baskets and sun dried pottery and began to paint and incise symbols on the rocks near their homes. Increased leisure time also led to the invention of games; gaming sticks have been found in many ruins.

Southern Utah's Land of Color is located on the northwest fringe of the area used by the Anasazi culture. A Basketmaker II site has been found in Zion Canyon, but if the modified Basketmaker people (Basketmaker III) ever lived here, they left little evidence behind, none of which has been discovered. However, in the Four Corners area—where Utah, Arizona, Colorado, and New Mexico meet—archeologists have identified a huge number of Basketmaker III sites.

Between A.D. 400 and 700, the Anasazi began to band together to form hamlets. Perhaps it was this tendency to congregate that caused the abandonment of peripheral sites, such as those in southern Utah. By the end of that period of coalescence, the Anasazi culture had advanced considerably. The people were starting to make more

sophisticated pithouses, to cultivate new varieties of corn, and to grow beans; they began to fire their pottery and to decorate it in a more sophisticated manner; and the bow and arrow replaced the atlatl as the principal weapon for hunting.

PUEBLOS

So great were the changes that occurred in the Anasazi Basketmaker III period that, although there were no signs of conflict, archeologists originally thought the Basketmakers had been replaced by an entirely new people. It is still unclear what caused these changes, but it is generally supposed that increased contact with other groups in the Southwest brought in new ideas. One important development was the adoption of cradle boards for carrying the young. These boards deformed the shape of the soft infant skull to such a degree that the long-headed Basketmakers eventually gave way to Anasazi with short, wide skulls. They were dubbed Pueblo people, taken from the Spanish word *pueblo*, meaning "community" or "village."

The Pueblo period has been divided into Pueblo 1 (A.D. 700 to 900), Pueblo II (A.D. 900 to 1100), and Pueblo III (A.D. 1100 to 1300). While there is little evidence to substantiate the existence of the earlier Pueblo I group in southern Utah, there are many signs indicating the presence of Puebloans of the later periods.

In the earliest Pueblo period, the Anasazi abandoned their pithouses and replaced them with dwellings made from poles interwoven with brush and mud, known as *jacal*, which they began to build above ground. Pithouses were incorporated into these new dwellings as ceremonial chambers, or *kivas*. Storage cists were now also built above ground entirely of slabs.

By the time the Pueblo II culture appeared in southern Utah, all buildings were of masonry construction, consisting of rows of stones mortared together with mud and hand plastered. Small, one-story dwellings were built in convenient places, such as beneath arches in the canyon walls, or on hilltops where they commanded a good view of the surrounding terrain. One extended family or clan is thought to have been represented at each site or community.

KIVAS

The only structures to remain below ground were the kivas, and these sometimes were only partially subterranean. Southern Utah's circular kivas are small, measuring between 12 and 15 feet across. One theory is that kivas were mainly used by Anasazi men as places to conduct important crop and/or religious ceremonies, to discuss community matters, and as workplaces. However, in the Four Corners area at that time, Great Kivas, associated with the Anasazi Chacoan culture, which ruled the San Juan basin, were used for large community gatherings by Chacoans traveling great distances throughout the area. The kiva was entered by descending a ladder through the roof, which was made from *vigas*, or beams, crisscrossed with smaller branches, and covered with adobe. Every kiva had a smoke hole, a deflector, and a small hole in the floor called a *sipapu*. The sipapu symbolizes the place where the Anasazi believed their ancestors emerged from a previous world. Today's southwestern Pueblo people consider themselves to be descendants of the Anasazi and still hold many beliefs in common with their ancestors; kivas continue to be the focus of ceremonial activities in the pueblo.

Anasazi ceramics, which varied from place to place, have been used by 20th-century archeologists as one of the principal means of dating and locating the different groups of Anasazi found in the Southwest. This pottery was both utilitarian and ornamental. Although the pottery designs differed between groups, they consisted chiefly of simple black designs on a white background. Black-on-red and red-on-orange designs have also been found. The exteriors of cooking vessels were often corregated with the thumbnail and left unpainted. Sand replaced fibers as a tempering and binding material for the pottery, and fur gave way to feathers in the fabrication of robes.

The Pueblo II people began to vary their burial rituals. The position for burial became less flexed, and included with the body were two or three items of pottery. Some bodies were interred in refuse pits, in abandoned houses, or under storage pits, with the children often being buried under the floors of dwellings. These practices indicate perhaps that the Anasazi considered all of the ground on which the village was built to be sacred.

By the 1100s, the great classical period of Pueblo culture was developing in the Four Corners area, but the Pueblo Indians of southern Utah were beginning to move on, perhaps because of increased cyclical drought in this marginal land, diminishing resources, and the desire for a better life elsewhere. They left considerable evidence behind them: sites have been discovered from Paragonah south along the west base of the Markagunt Plateau, along Kanab Creek, the Paria River, and the Rio Virgin and its tributaries. Northwest of Parowan, arrowheads and a number of petroglyphs (incised rock art) suggest that the Anasazi, at least for a time, used the terraces of the high plateaus as a hunting ground.

In the northeastern portion of southern Utah's Land of Color another contemporaneous culture, known as the Fremont, has been identified by archeologists. The Fremont were originally thought to be Anasazi, but are now considered to be a separate culture with some relationship to the Anasazi. Strong evidence of their existence was found at Capitol Reef National Park in south-central Utah, leading archeologists to name the culture after the Fremont River, the river that traverses the area. The Fremont did more hunting and gathering than the Anasazi and did not usually live in above-ground masonry structures, as a rule preferring to remain in pithouses. The kiva was not part of their tradition. They evolved a unique piece of footwear, with a heel made from the dewclaw of a deer, which probably allowed a better grip on slippery surfaces. But the greatest difference between the cultures may be seen in the rock art the Fremont left behind. Fremont petroglyphs and pictographs tend to be large and elaborate, often including bejeweled trapezoidal figures and colorful shields. In the 14th century, the Fremont mysteriously disappeared. Whether they joined the Anasazi in their migration to

Anasazi kiva, Anasazi Indian Village State Park

An Indian Legend

The Paiute people originally had no written language, consequently, their explanations of the various mysteries of nature have been passed from one generation to the next by word of mouth. Fortunately, these simple but extremely fascinating tales were secured from the Paiutes by the late Mr. William R. Palmer of Cedar City who published them in a small volume entitled Why The North Star Stands Still. *The book has recently been reissued by Zion Natural History Association. The following story, which indicates that the Paiutes probably witnessed the last volcanic eruptions in southern Utah about 1,000 years ago, is reprinted with the consent of the author's family and the publisher.*

How Whistler and Badger Got Their Homes

Long, long ago before trouble was made among the animals, e-am-pit, the whistler, and oo-nam-put, the badger, were good friends. They were also cousins, and they went everywhere together, always making their camp under the same tree. They tried to do the same things, but badger was always the stronger when they played their contest games.

Whistler, though, was the best singer and his call could be heard a long way in the forest. Badger could scarcely make any noise and he envied e-am-pit's

shrill but cheery whistle as its peal went echoing up the canyons in the early morning silence. Sometimes there was a speck of bitterness in oo-nam-put's jealousy. When the whistler saw that, he always said, "Friend badger, I would be glad to trade my whistle for your fur coat," and that healed the sore and made them good friends again.

But a time came when trouble arose between them that made them enemies forever after. When they grew up they both wanted the same wife. E-am-pit went out early in the morning and made the woods ring with his music, but oo-nam-put snuggled up and protected her from the cold winds. She decided that she liked the comfort of oo-nam-put's fur better than whistler's music, so she married him.

One day the badger left home and climbed to the very top of a high peak. He could see the country for a long distance in every direction. Just when he was enjoying the sights the most he saw something that almost stopped his heart. He saw e-am-pit running off with his wife and he knew he could not run fast enough to catch them.

The old badger flew into a great rage. He began turning and twisting around, and he tried to screech at the runaway couple, but he had no voice and the sounds he made were so puny that they mocked him. Then he began furiously

to scratch and claw the earth. He was throwing dirt and rocks with all his might and with every foot. He was too angry to notice that he was digging a hole and sinking himself deeper and deeper into the ground. He clawed like a maniac, and the rocks were coming furiously up from the bottom of the pit. They came banging and clashing against each other, then went rolling off down the steep hillside.

The whistler and the badger's wife saw that oo-nam-put was not running after them, so they stopped to watch and to laugh at the way he was throwing rocks.

Now those rocks were all filled with fire and when they clashed together they threw out their sparks, which fell like a shower back into the hole. All at once the hole caught fire and with one great belch from below poor old oo-nam-put was thrown out. Bruised and burned, he was heaved up into the air, then falling hard, he went rolling off down the hillside. The fire kept shooting upward in a bigger and bigger stream. It was throwing out more rocks than the poor jealous old badger ever could throw. The rocks now were molten and came oozing down the side of the mountain like red-hot mud. It was so hot that the trees and brush and everything in its path were burned up in an instant. The badger saw it moving toward him, and forgetting his anger he fled the scene as fast as his tired old legs could carry him.

Now whistler saw the molten stream moving slowly down the valley and knew that something must be done to stop it. He pouched out his sides and his cheeks and blew with all his might upon it. He saw the molten lava wrinkle and creep more slowly as it cooled. He ran along and blew frantically upon it until it came to a full stop. He kept on blowing all winter and at last saw it freeze and break up like big blocks of ice.

The vain old whistler thought his blowing had done it. He swelled all up with pride and imagined himself a great fellow. He led the animals up and down along the lava flow and showed them that he blew here, and he blew here, and he blew here.

Shinob, the god, grew tired of hearing the vain old fellow boast. He called the whistler to him and said, "E-am-pit, that was a big thing you did to make all these black rocks. Now nobody likes this place or wants to live around here. Only you are happy here. You should be here all the time to tell the living things that come around how you made it. I am giving you these black rocks for your home. You can crawl down under them, and no one else will ever want to come and live here with you.

Because the badger lost his temper and brought on such disaster, Shinob was angry with him also. The god showed him the country he had spoiled and asked him why he had done it. Oo-nam-put said, "I was mad when I was digging that hole. I was too angry to see how fast I was throwing rocks. I am scared to go in holes any more, and all my life I will stay out of them. I will never go in holes any more." Shinob said, "Oo-nam-put, you lost your temper and set the world on fire. You are afraid now to go in holes for fear you might get thrown out again. Now your home forever must be a hole in the ground. You will dig it with fear, but you will go easy and gently, and you will always be afraid to get angry in there. You will be safe because you will be afraid to get angry and set your hole on fire again."

And so from that day to this the whistler's home has been in the lava flow, and the badger has been digging his burrow in the earth. Both have come to like their homes and are glad to crawl into them when storms come and the cold winds of winter blow. They may be neighbors, but they refuse ever again to be friends. Oo-nam-put is a shy, surly, ill-tempered fellow who snaps and snarls at everyone who comes near him. Unhappy is the poor fellow on whom he once sets his iron jaws.

As for e-am-pit, when the sun shines he comes out on the big rocks in his dooryard and still sends his cherry whistle echoing down the country.

the more fertile Little Colorado and Rio Grande drainages farther southwest, or emerged as the Shoshone, Ute, or Southern Paiute cultures, is still unclear.

THE SOUTHERN PAIUTES

Before the arrival of Europeans in the West, there were estimated to be 18,000 Paiutes living in their aboriginal homeland. The Paiutes belong to the Shoshonean language group, which relates them to the Shoshone and Ute cultures. The name Ute is Navajo for "upper," because the Ute people were the "upper people" or "hill dwellers." The name Paiute, sometimes spelled Piute, means "water Utes" (from *pah*, meaning "water").

The "Yutas," as Spanish explorer Father Silvestre Velez de Escalante called them in his 1776 diary, once inhabited a vast territory in the West, which stretched from the Colorado River in northern Arizona as far as southern California, encompassing the Arizona Strip, southern Utah, southern Nevada, and much of southern California. Part of this area is referred to as the Great Basin. Their homeland has been described as desolate and inhospitable, but the Paiutes were at home there, with the environment dictating the Paiute lifestyle and population.

Although, on the surface, southern Utah's landscape did not seem to offer much besides sparse vegetation and spectacular scenery, the Paiutes knew how to make the best use of the geography of the region. They were resourceful nomads living off the land, much like the Desert Archaic people who had preceded them thousands of years before. During the summer, they enjoyed the high plateau and its many different foodstuffs. When winter came, they migrated to the desert.

FOOD AND CLOTHING

In 1776, when the Spanish Dominguez-Escalante expedition first encountered the Paiutes while searching for a route back to Santa Fe, the natives were growing maize in fields irrigated by the rivers, as well as hunting animals and gathering wild foods. The Paiutes probably had expert knowledge of native plants and had much in common with the Anasazi before them, using every edible plant, seed, and root. Finely woven baskets of all kinds demonstrate that the Paiutes were, and continue to be, excellent artisans (the William R. Palmer Collection of Paiute baskets and other artifacts on display at Iron Mission State Park and at Southern Utah University in Cedar City, is well worth searching out). Although tightly woven and beautifully designed, Paiute basketry was principally utilitarian and used for gathering plants and seeds, waterproofed with piñon pitch for transporting water, and even served as headgear. Piñon nuts were a nutritious and tasty delicacy in the fall, but the rest of the year, ants, grasshoppers, lizards, birds, rabbits, and fish made up the Paiutes' varied diet. Larger game animals, such as deer, were killed with bows and arrows.

Because a Paiute's life was seminomadic, permanent homes were unnecessary. Brush

shelters, known to Anglos as wickiups, were erected wherever camp was set up. These were taken down when the time came to move on. The ability of the Paiutes to adapt to their environment accounted for their resilience and survival. They made special clothes to meet the changing seasons and different camp locations. Much of the year, clothing was minimal, but in cooler weather clothing made from rabbit skin or buckskin sewn together with yucca fibers provided warmth. Like the Anasazi, the Paiutes used yucca fibers to make sandals.

Southern Utah was one of the last areas in the West to be explored by Euroamericans. Although the Dominguez-Escalante expedition and several explorations in the early 1800s had little impact on the Paiutes, the native way of life was changed forever by the arrival, in 1847, of the first Mormon settlers in Utah and the discovery of gold in California in 1848. The Mormons began to establish their southern Utah "Indian missions" on or near strategic Paiute water sources, and they turned their large herds of domesticated animals loose on aboriginal and traditional gathering areas. The white settlers were initially welcomed by the Paiutes, who were interested in the newcomers' farming methods and religious beliefs; but unforeseen competition for resources led to tension between the two groups. This conflict of interest finally led to a decline in the traditional Paiute way of life and their rapid dependence on the new arrivals—a state of affairs resented by both sides.

The Paiutes were a peaceable people; however, even before the arrival of white settlers, conflict between them and the Utes and Navajos who also used the region caused problems. The Utes and Navajos had obtained horses from the Spanish in the 1600s, allowing the two well-organized

groups to put pressure on hunter-gatherer tribes such as the Paiutes, whose affiliations were principally familial, not tribal. Although related to the Paiutes, the Utes nevertheless extracted a yearly tribute from them, which when it could not be paid in beads, hides, or some other desired object, was exacted by taking Paiute children as slaves. These slaves were traded with the Spanish (and later with the Navajo) in a thriving business that was to cause escalating conflict, as Mormon settlers, committed to the abolition of slavery, entered the arena. The Navajo also periodically raided the Paiutes from across the Colorado River, but, in fact, the relationship between the Navajos and Paiutes alternated between clashes and cooperation, as the western frontier increasingly fell into white hands.

DECLINE OF THE PAIUTES

In the late 1800s, there were many attempts by the federal government and local Mormon communities to move the Paiutes. With the decimation of their traditional food sources and restrictive occupation of their homeland, tribal members were given little choice but to try to adapt to the Anglo way of life. The government appeared set on absorbing the country's American Indians into the general population, thereby forcing Indians to adopt what was being promoted as an "American" lifestyle. Traditional American Indian homelands were seized by the government and sold cheaply to homesteaders, with the argument that the native people were not using the land to its fullest potential. During the widespread Indian Wars, which spanned several decades in the late 1800s, the government forced many American Indian tribes onto reservations in an effort to control them and indoctrinate them into

European mores. One of the most significant actions was to force Indian children to attend boarding schools far away from their families and to forbid them to speak their native tongue or to dress traditionally. This practice, which lasted until the 1950s and still occurs to some degree, has had a tremendous impact on American Indian cultures, since tribal elders have frequently been unable to pass on the traditional practices that have sustained individual tribes for many centuries. All of these things particularly affected the Paiutes, whose cultural traditions were less strongly identified than were those of many other tribes. The Paiute population and its land holdings declined drastically, despite futile efforts by the federal government and the Mormon Church to ameliorate the situation.

THE PAVEMENT OF GOOD INTENTIONS

With the general abolition of forced schooling in the fifties, the government tried another method of moving American Indians into mainstream American culture. The hope was that by forcing certain smaller tribes to lose their legal cultural identity, the native people would have little choice but to integrate into the general population. The loss of legal Indian status was to have a devastating effect on the 3 percent of America's Indian tribes who were terminated. Senator Watkins of Utah was one of the original sponsors of the Termination Bill. Under its terms, two Indian tribes from Utah were affected: a small, select group of northern Utes and the southern Paiutes. Although the Paiutes did not meet the criteria for termination, they found themselves ineligible for government services provided by the Bureau of Indian Affairs. Payment of back taxes was required on former reservation land.

Over the next 25 years, the Paiutes lost much of their land, culture, and pride. Finally, after proving to the government that termination had not worked, many of the terminated tribes across the country sought reinstatement, or federal recognition. In 1980, the Paiutes once more became a federally recognized tribe, known as the Paiute Indian Tribe of Southern Utah, which has its headquarters in Cedar City, Utah. Today, the Paiutes inhabit three states, with a number living on the approximately 500,000 acres that make up the Shivwits and Kaibab-Paiute reservations, and many others living off reservation. Despite numerous attempts to remove and to acculturate the tribe into the American mainstream, members of the tribe have stood fast and have fought to retain their way of life. The Paiute people are continuing to make strides in strengthening their ties with one another, improving their educational attainment and caring for the overall wellbeing of every tribal member through a variety of programs. The tribe celebrates reinstatement at the annual Paiute Restoration Gathering, which is held every June in Cedar City.

SPANISH EXPLORATION OF UTAH

The first Europeans to visit southern Utah were Spaniards exploring the vast territory of the Southwest that, led by Coronado, in 1540, they had claimed for the Spanish Crown. At first, the Spanish concentrated their colonization efforts on New Mexico and Arizona. Later, however, they began to journey farther afield, exploring canyon country that had previously seemed impenetrable. In July 1776, Padres Silvestre Velez de Escalante and Francisco Atanasio Dominguez and party left the

Spanish capital of Santa Fe, New Mexico, in an attempt to find a land route between that mission and one in Monterey, California. The Franciscan friars entered Utah near Jensen, on the Green River, skirted the southern base of the Uintah Mountains, passed Utah Lake, and continued south toward Utah's Dixie. Before reaching the Rio Virgin, which they called the Rio Sulfureo, for the sulphur springs that are located just above the crossing, their Ute Indian guide deserted them. With the approaching winter, dwindling supplies and unknown risks to the west, they abandoned their California quest and began their return to Santa Fe.

The tired and hungry explorers worked their way around the base of the Vermilion Cliffs, crossed the creek south of Kanab, and, after many unsuccessful attempts to find a way to cross the Grand Canyon, finally forded the Colorado River at what was later called the Crossing of the Fathers. Today, this site is inundated by Lake Powell and is known as Padre Bay.

Spanish explorations of the Southwest were frequently extremely well documented in diaries and sketches kept by members of the expeditions. The Dominguez-Escalante expedition was no exception. It remains a landmark event in Utah's history because Father Escalante was the first European to describe the country and the native people of Utah. The diary he kept about his journey

continues to provide historians with important information about early exploration of the region, the attitudes and feelings of the explorers, and the sources for many of Utah's place names.

SMITH COMPLETES THE OLD SPANISH TRAIL

Fifty years passed, then, in 1821, Mexico's independence from Spain brought about a general Spanish exodus from North America and Mexican acquisition of lands previously held by Spain. After years of Spanish repression and protectionism, Mexico was eager to link the East Coast to the West, thereby improving communications and allowing a greater variety of trade items to flow back and forth across the country. This led immediately to the opening of the Santa Fe Trail, a trading route between Franklin, Missouri, and Santa Fe, New Mexico. Explorers, traders, a few settlers, and others seeking their fortune in the vast new western territory began to follow the often-dangerous trail to the West.

One of the earliest of these frontiersmen was Jedediah Strong Smith, a God-fearing and resolute fur trapper and explorer. In 1826, he left Great Salt Lake, followed the Sevier River to Clear Creek, crossed over the mountains to where Cove Fort now stands, and traveled south along the present site of Interstate 15, until he encountered the Rio Virgin.

Smith and his men followed the Virgin to

its junction with the Colorado, and thence into California, thereby establishing a trading trail all the way to the Pacific Ocean. On his return trip across the Nevada Desert, Smith nearly died from thirst and hunger. In 1827 he again traversed the state, following much the same path as before, except that in the Dixie area he left the Rio Virgin to discover an easier route.

Two years later, between 1829 and 1830, Antonio Armijo led a trading expedition over Escalante's return trail, via the Crossing of the Fathers to the Rio Virgin, and thence to California, following the path of Smith's second journey. Also in 1830, William Wolfskill organized a party of trappers in Santa Fe and led them through eastern Utah to the Sevier, where they picked up Smith's trail. This expedition, the account of which is preserved in the writings of George C. Yount, a member of the party, is the only record of travel in the 1830s, aside from that of Armijo. It is quite certain, however, that during the next 10 to 15 years a number of caravans from Santa Fe made their way to Green River, down Salina Canyon to the Sevier, then followed this stream into Panguitch Valley, thence across the plateau to Red Creek (Paragonah), and continued south into California.

During those years of travel along the Old Spanish Trail (later called the Old Mormon Trail), names were given to Santa Clara Creek, La Verkin Creek, the Rio Virgin, and the Sevier River. It is ironic that the Old Spanish Trail, which was blazed by the Dominguez-Escalante expedition, was never actually used by the Spanish thereafter; however, it was to be of tremendous benefit to the flood of people migrating west.

THE MORMONS

In 1844, U.S. Army Captain John C. Fremont came up the Old Spanish Trail, making careful notes as he traveled, and wrote the first scientific report on the country surrounding the route. When the United States government released this narrative, a copy was secured by high officials of the Church of Jesus Christ of Latter-day Saints.

The LDS Church, formed in 1830, was also known as the "Mormon" Church because of its emphasis on the teaching of the Book of Mormon, which was revealed to Joseph Smith between 1823 and 1830. Latter-day Saints believe that prophets like Smith have restored true Christian teachings "in these latter days," and they follow both the Bible and the Book of Mormon. The Church has a membership of more than 8 million worldwide and requires of its members belief, service, tithing (10 percent of an individual's profits are given annually to the Church), and obedience to church authorities. Since Mormons believe that families can remain together forever, there is a natural emphasis on protecting the family unit. The temple plays a key role in a Mormon's life, since it is here that education and sacred rituals reinforce his or her faith.

When Mormon elders obtained Fremont's report, they had strong reasons for the careful study they gave its contents. Their history in the East had not been a happy one. Persecuted by officials and others, they had been forced to move from New York state into Ohio and Missouri. At that time, they were located in Nauvoo, Illinois, where they were again engaged in serious conflict with nonbelievers who felt threatened by Mormon beliefs. In 1844, when Church President Joseph Smith was murdered by an angry mob in Carthage, Illinois, it became evident to the succeeding church president, Brigham Young, that if the Mormon Church were to survive, with any measure of peace and security, a move to a more secure location would be necessary. No doubt the Fremont report figured importantly in the Mormons choosing Utah as a place where they could find shelter, live off the land, and establish their own territory.

There are numerous accounts of the long and hazardous trek the Mormons made across the plains before reaching Salt Lake Valley. Many were buried on the prairies, and those who did survive were firmly bound into a political, economic, and ecclesiastical unit, which was to prove essential in their battle with the inhospitable land in which they had chosen to dwell.

THIS IS THE PLACE

The advance guard of the Mormon migration reached Salt Lake Valley on July 21, 1847. When the main body of the first group arrived three days later, on July 24, Brigham Young looked over the pristine valley and uttered the historic phrase, "This is the place." To this day, Pioneer Day is celebrated every July 24 by the residents of Utah, who often reenact the sighting of Salt Lake City by the Mormon pioneers, hold parades and competitions, and lay on a feast of traditional pioneer food and drink, and displays of handicrafts.

At the time the Mormons first arrived here, Utah was part of uninhabited Mexican territory. In 1846, the United States government, spurred by favorable reports about the rich resources waiting to be exploited in the vast western territories, embarked on a war with Mexico for these untapped lands. They were joined in this endeavor by a group of 549 Mormon soldiers, known as the Mormon Battalion, who marched 2,000 miles from Iowa to southern California to assist in the war, but never saw action. In 1848, the Treaty of Guadalupe-Hidalgo ceded much of the Southwest to the United States, thereby encouraging many people in search of a fortune and a new start to make the long journey west along the Santa Fe Trail and the Old Spanish Trail. Brigham Young planned to claim a vast area of the West as the Mormon State of Deseret, but the government had other plans. Deseret never became a reality; instead, the Mormons, who longed for a home of their own, found themselves part of the new American territory of Utah (named for the Ute Indians who lived here).

It was soon clear that the Salt Lake Valley was not large enough to accommodate the great body of Latter-day Saints who were slowly but persistently migrating westward. In addition to those people exiled from the midwestern states, an increasing number of converts came from other parts of America and from Europe to seek refuge here. Therefore, in 1849, Brigham Young directed Parley P. Pratt to organize an expedition to study the areas lying to the south, with a view to colonizing them. Although, in 1847, Young had sent a party led by Jefferson Hunt to the Pacific Coast for supplies, he was not satisfied with Hunt's report on southern Utah.

Parley P. Pratt's company of nearly 50 men left Fort Provo in late November, journeyed south following the approximate route of today's Highway 89 to the north end of Panguitch Valley, and followed the Old Spanish Trail to Birch Creek,

which was to become Parowan, the first town in southern Utah. Part of the group remained there to recuperate and to care for their animals, but others pushed south into Utah's Dixie.

On the Santa Clara River, they picked up Jefferson Hunt's trail, followed it through the Mountain Meadows, noted the iron deposits west of the present town of Cedar City, and rejoined the expedition at Birch Creek. On their arduous return to Salt Lake City, they passed through the sites of the present towns of Beaver and Fillmore. The Mormon Church based its plans for the colonization of southern Utah on Pratt's report.

SYSTEMATIC COLONIZATION

Colonization within the territory was carefully planned and executed. Groups of men, handpicked by church leaders, were directed to make systematic exploration of a region in a similar fashion to Pratt's company and to search out places where communities might be built. Although this generally resolved itself into a search for water—a most precious resource in this semiarid land—soil, fuel, building materials, mineral resources, native vegetation, temperature, and other factors were studied and noted in the reports.

Following the selection of suitable sites, the Church organized companies of men with specific skills to colonize them. While volunteers were accepted, a significant part of each company was "called" by the Church. The "call" generally came to the pioneers unexpectedly and usually consisted of a reading of their names by church authorities at the general conference held in Salt Lake City. Sometimes, however, for the benefit of those who could not attend the conference, local newspapers published their names, or the authori-

ties sent a note informing them of their selection. As there was nothing mandatory in the "call," all were free to reject it. The fact that few did so can be attributed to any one of several factors, or perhaps a combination of them: an unquestioned confidence in the church leadership, a willingness to sacrifice individually for the good of all, and a devout belief that in accepting they were fulfilling a mission for the Church and for God.

While the personal wishes of those chosen to colonize a new area apparently were not considered, their training and skills were carefully scrutinized. Isolation would of necessity require that each community be as self-sufficient as possible. To attain this end, the church elders had to plan most carefully. An understanding of the method used to acquire this balance can best be obtained by studying the occupations of part of those "called" for the Cotton Mission to Utah's Dixie in 1861. The list reads in part as follows: 31 farmers, 1 horticulturist, 2 gardeners, 2 vine dressers, 1 vintner, 1 distiller, 2 with molasses mills, 14 blacksmiths, 2 wheelwrights, 1 machinist, 1 mill builder, 2 millwrights, 3 millers, 10 coopers, 1 adobe maker, 5 masons, 1 plasterer, 1 painter, 3 carpenters, 1 turner, 1 joiner, 1 shingle maker, 3 cabinet makers, 1 chair maker, 2 wool carders, 1 weaver, 1 tailor, 1 hatter, 1 brush maker, 1 tanner, 5 shoemakers, 1 minerologist, 2 miners, 4 musicians, 1 fiddler, 3 school teachers, 4 clerks, 1 lawyer, 1 printer, 2 surveyors, 2 daguerreans (photographers), 1 butcher, 1 baker, 1 castor oil maker, 1 tobacco maker, 1 sailor, and 1 manufacturer who did not state his specific skill.

In addition to vocational training, other factors figured importantly. The most industrious, dependable, and courageous were needed to provide direction and coherence for each pioneer town. Often those whose diligence and ingenuity

Pioneer home in Parowan

were being rewarded by well-tilled fields, or producing orchards and comfortable homes, were asked to sell their holding and travel many miles to begin anew.

BUILDING A NEW COMMUNITY

Generally, the vanguard of each community traveled in a body. On arriving at their chosen spot, the colonizers surveyed their town and divided it into blocks and lots. With the choice of their homes left largely to chance, they accepted the locations as they drew them from a hat; however, people often traded among themselves when the drawing proved unsatisfactory.

To make sure that there would be food to eat, the first colonizers of a new town generally began to prepare the soil for planting right away. Because this took precedence over the construction of dwelling places, families lived in wagon boxes or crude dugouts until the men and boys could spare time to build better shelters. Cooperation was essential for the construction of dams, ditches, and the equitable distribution of the precious water. Often, the first year would see the settlers having to band together in the building of

a fort to protect themselves from attacks by native people upset about the loss of their traditional lands and resources. It is no marvel that these people lived so well together; it was necessary for their survival.

A fundamental part of the property of each community was its livestock, which consisted principally of horses and cattle. Until the settlers could build fences, they grazed their animals on nearby grasslands under the watchful eyes of herdsmen who were ordered to keep the herd intact, to prevent damage to crops, and to ensure that the stock was not taken by bands of renegade Indians who often raided the new settlements. These renegade groups consisted of small numbers of defiant Navajos left behind after the Long Walk of 1864, as well as unhappy Paiutes who were unwilling to see their traditional lands taken by Europeans. On occasion, when it seemed expedient to the Navajos, they would form an alliance with small numbers of Paiutes in the Arizona Strip area and raid together, thereby confusing the issue as to which native people were responsible for individual raids. As soon as possible, the colonists would erect fences with stones cleared from the farmland, but later on, they increasingly built stake and rider (rip gut) fences and log fences of various designs.

Prior to the construction of suitable buildings, the residents of a community held their public gatherings in branch-covered "boweries," large tents, or in some of the larger private homes. The earliest public buildings were "meeting houses" or chapels, which were used not only for ecclesiastical functions but also as schoolhouses and recreation centers. With the single exception of Silver Reef, the towns in southern Utah's Land of Color were devoid of saloons, gambling houses, and similar institutions.

THE PIONEER HOME

The basic unit of pioneer life was the home. Many of the first inhabitants of a new community lived in hastily built dugouts, but as soon as there was time, a determined effort was made to build better shelters. Since building materials were dictated by the nature of the immediate environment, the people constructed their homes of logs, sundried adobes, cut and uncut native stone, and, in a few places, of burned brick. The first dwellings were often built without floors, but these were installed as soon as circumstances permitted. The wooden floors were then strewn with straw and covered with home-woven or rag rugs. The windows of the home were usually filled in with isinglass or oiled parchment. Glass was a decided luxury. The lack of screening material over doors and windows added considerably to the ill health of early colonists.

Beds were made from native materials. Straw or corn husks provided adequate mattresses unless, perchance, someone neglectfully included a corn cob. Feather-filled ticks, which accumulated very slowly, were prized items (Brigham Young's original corn husk mattress may be seen, along with other items from pioneer homes, at St. George's Pioneer Museum). Clothing, hats, and shoes were usually manufactured locally, and the women spent many hours carding, spinning, weaving, and dyeing woolen materials. The production of cotton in what was known as Utah's Dixie (named after the cotton-growing region in the South), and the resulting factory at Washington, benefitted everyone.

A substantial stone fireplace, a standard feature of most dwellings, provided not only light and heat but its glowing embers were used by early pioneers to cook many of their meals. The people gathered piñon pine, juniper, cottonwood, and sometimes driftwood from the streams for fuel. Although primitive lights, known as "bitches," were contrived by immersing wicks in animal fats, the successful introduction of sheep and production of tallow enabled the settlers to make candles.

Brooms were made by hand, using willows, broom cane, or broom straw. Soap was obtained from the roots of the oose, or yucca, a plant used extensively by the native people of the Southwest, or by boiling animal fats with suitable alkaline salts. These salts were extracted from cottonwood trees by immersing their white ash in vats of water. Sometimes, when animal fats were scarce, the people gathered the grease from their dishpans and saved it for soap manufacture. For more on the pioneer way of life, Juanita Brooks's excellent autobiographical book, *Quicksand and Cactus*, provides a fascinating remembrance of Mormon life at the turn of the century.

During the early periods of colonization, food shortages due to poor harvests and depradations by insects sometimes became critical as evidenced by the numerous records of the consumption of pigweed greens, sego lily bulbs, and other edible native plants. Few communities are without a record of a "starving time." Preservation of crops was an annual problem. While root vegetables could easily be kept in bins, many staples could be preserved only by the more tedious process of dehydration. Consequently, dried vegetables, fruit, and meat (jerky) became an essential part of a Mormon's daily rations. Some of the fruit was preserved by placing it in large stone crocks and covering it with molasses, which was made from Chinese sorghum cane. Residents of Toquerville and Short Creek (Colorado City) were particularly successful with this practice.

Such circumstances dictated that each member of the family lend a hand to ensure the preservation and comfort of all. Everyone was assigned a job, according to size, age, and skills. This interdependence created families who were particularly closely knit.

COMMON PROBLEMS

In addition to the problems naturally inherent in establishing a home in a new land, the southern Utah pioneers, from time to time, faced special difficulties. Some years drought made water conservation vital, but then the next season might bring disastrous floods caused by torrential rains. These raging floods are common to desert country, but they were new to the pioneers, who were mostly of European origin. Overgrazing by livestock compounded the problem of erosion and was the reason for the demise of a number of Mormon settlements. Nearly every town suffered crop damage as a result of insect depredations for which the settlers were ill-prepared.

In addition, the settling of Utah by whites put pressure on American Indian groups such as the Utes, Paiutes, and Navajo, who already had a history of alternately cooperating and fighting each other over resources. The practices of the Mormons, who were committed to working every piece of available land, were at odds with those of American Indians, who emphasized conservation of resources. Despite the commitment of the Mormon Church to converting the Indians and teaching them European practices, resentment continued to grow towards whites throughout the late 1800s.

Between the date of the first southern Utah settlement (1851) and the turn of the century, several events occurred that affected nearly everyone in this area. In 1852, the territorial legislature passed an act forbidding anyone to take Indians as slaves. For some time several Ute tribes had been in the habit of raiding weaker Indians and selling their captives in New Mexico. The enforcement of this act, coupled with a general dissatisfaction with white encroachment, laid the foundation for the Indian rebellion led by Ute Chief Walker (Wakara) in Sanpete County to the north. The Walker War, as it was known, led to a general mobilization of the Mormon communities in the south and to the building of fortresses throughout the territory.

A climate of fear and anxiety arose among the members of the Mormon community as a result of clashes with their native neighbors and the belief that the federal government was sending in an army to take over their hard-fought territory. These pressures led, in 1857, to the darkest event in Mormon history. On September 11 of that year, a group of Mormon militiamen, principally from the early pioneer town of Cedar City, acting under the command of their military superiors, and accompanied by a large band of local Indians, surrounded a party of white immigrants from Missouri and Arkansas and its army escort, as they rested at the Mountain Meadows before continuing their journey to California. Incensed by reports that the immigrants had unceremoniously demanded food and made abusive remarks about them and their leaders, the Mormons and their Indian cohorts attacked the party, killing more than 120 of the people and sparing only 17 young children.

The consequences of this tragic event were far-reaching. A federal investigation attempted for many years to bring to justice those responsible for the massacre. In 1876, John D. Lee, one of southern Utah's earliest and most respected pioneers, gave himself up after years of hiding out as a ferryman at Lee's Ferry on the Colorado River. He was tried, found guilty, and subsequently executed in March 1877, at the spot where the Mountain Meadows massacre took place. It is generally acknowledged that by giving himself up to the government, in the certain knowledge that he would be found guilty and executed, John D. Lee sought to atone for the sins of his fellow Mormons and to prevent them from being further persecuted. In that he was indeed successful, for the other perpetrators, who had fled Cedar City, leading to a decline in its population in the years following the massacre, were never tried. Many of their names are found in the records of a number of southern Utah villages settled after 1857. In 1990, a simple granite monument bearing the names of those who were murdered was erected at the Mountain Meadows.

Over the years, the Mormon community has sought to understand and come to terms with this sad legacy, which continues to be a source of deep reflection to this day. An excellent discussion of the circumstances surrounding the Mountain Meadows affair is contained in Juanita Brooks's 1950 book, *The Mountain Meadow Massacre*, published by the University of Oklahoma Press.

Between December 1861 and January 1862, the region was visited by the heaviest rains in its recorded history. Most accounts say the Great Rain lasted for 40 days. The most conservative statement maintains that rain fell daily for 28 days. Streams swelled to bursting point, overflowed their banks, and did considerable damage. Laboriously constructed dams and irrigation ditches were destroyed. The ground became a veritable quagmire, with farmlands washed away and animals perishing before they could extricate themselves. Adobe buildings simply melted to nothing. Although there are no positive records to show how much rain fell, the severity of the storm and the damage it wrought is undeniable. A number of communities in the Virgin River Valley, such as the one at Grafton, were washed away completely and had to be relocated on higher ground or abandoned completely.

THE MUDDY MISSION

In 1864, church leaders issued a "call" for volunteers to settle along the Muddy Creek in what is now Nevada. The following year, the settlers moved to that place and began building a number of villages as part of the Muddy Mission. That year also saw the start of the Blackhawk War. For some time, the Indians had been resisting being placed on reservations by the U.S. government. When a number of American Indians died at Gunnison, Sanpete County, of the western disease of smallpox, against which they had no immunity, the Indians blamed the Mormon settlers for their troubles. In a council called to resolve the problems, an indiscreet settler, reputedly drunk, insulted a tribal leader and pulled him from his horse. This incident was all that was needed to set off hostilities between the Mormons and the native people. For three years the conflict raged, leading to the deaths of at least 70 whites and an unknown number of American Indians. In southern Utah, the residents of small settlements were advised by the Church to join larger communities, to build forts, and to desert many outposts. Despite doing this, the men from many abandoned settlements traveled great distances each day to tend their crops and to protect their livestock. After the war ended, the towns were frequently resettled.

In May 1866, Congress passed an act granting to Nevada a portion of what had for-merly been part of the Utah territory. With a scarcity of survey lines making accurate definition of the proposed boundaries impossible, the settlers on the Muddy Creek found their political status somewhat questionable. Some held that they were in Arizona, while others thought they were still part of Utah. Nevada officials maintained that they belonged to that state. In the years that followed, the residents of the Muddy Mission continued to pay taxes to Utah.

In 1869, when a survey carried out by Major John Wesley Powell substantiated Nevada's claim, that state promptly requested payment of back taxes. The Nevada legislature further complicated the problem by demanding that all taxes be paid in coin, a scarce item among the Mormons. Church leaders advised the settlers to abandon their homes and to return to Utah. In December 1870, at a mass meeting called to resolve the issue, the settlers accepted the counsel as being the best solution to their dilemma. Early in 1871, therefore, about 600 people began the exodus from Nevada to Utah. Many of those fleeing the Muddy Mission arrived in Long Valley, where they were taken in by several communities and given help in starting over.

In 1874, shortly before his death, Brigham Young inaugurated the United Order of Enoch, an experiment in communal living, in most of the towns of southern Utah. The United Order met with varying degrees of success, mainly because the system required that all assets be shared by the community—a bitter pill for those who had mastered this rugged land and built successful farming operations. The United Order was most successful at Orderville, in Long Valley, where it found favor among residents consisting largely of recent arrivals from the Muddy Mission; the system lasted here for the better part of a decade.

POLYGAMY OUTLAWED

In 1882, Congress passed the Edmunds Act defining polygamous marriage as a felony and polygamous living as a misdemeanor. Anyone found guilty of either was fined and disenfranchised. An antipolygamy act, passed some 20 years before had proved ineffective, and even the Poland Act of 1874, which gave control of the courts to the federal judiciary, had not solved the government's problem. In 1884, however, a test case involving the Edmunds Act was carried to the Supreme Court. When that body declared the act valid, federal officials began a concerted effort to stamp out the practice.

The practice of polygamy was one of the tenets of the Mormon religion; however, according to *Utah, a Guide to the State*, published by Hastings House in 1941, the number of Mormons subscribing to the principles of polygamous living has always been overestimated. Levi Edgar Young, a church authority and historian, places the figure at 3 percent of marriageable adults, while Bernard de Voto, a critic of the Mormons, estimates it at perhaps 2 percent. Despite this, the entire Mormon community joined in protecting those of its members practicing polygamy when the "Feds" came. Congress retaliated in 1887 with the passage of the Edmunds-Tucker Act, which provided, among other things, for the disincorporation of the LDS Church and the confiscation of most of its property, unless polygamy was discontinued.

In 1890 a fourth president of the Church was appointed. Sensing the futility of continued resistance, this new leader, Wilford Woodruff, issued a manifesto advising all Mormons to abstain from the practice of polygamy. At the general conference held in October the membership concurred with the decision.

GROWTH FOLLOWS THE MANIFESTO

Following the adoption of the manifesto and adherence to its principles, the largely Mormon state of Utah was able to make more rapid progress. The president of the United States pardoned those who had been imprisoned and restored their civil rights. Citizens made a concerted move for long-denied statehood and, on January 4, 1896, Utah became the 45th state in the Union.

Significant changes have taken place in southern Utah since the turn of the century. The lack of understanding about the carrying capacity of the rangelands and watersheds, and the overgrazing that resulted, led to a considerable reduction in the income derived from livestock raising. As a result, federal agencies like the Bureau of Land Management (BLM) were created to supervise and control grazing on public lands, leading to a partial restoration of the range.

Over the years, southern Utah's unique environment has been recognized and cared for in other ways, too. The infrastructure of this remote part of the state has steadily improved, with the construction of new roads and public facilities. An unprecedented number of natural and historic areas have been set aside in southern Utah's Land of Color, including Zion, Bryce Canyon, Capitol Reef, and Arizona's Grand Canyon national parks; Cedar Breaks and Pipe Spring national monuments; as well as eight state parks and two national forests. Construction of the Glen Canyon Dam in the 1960s, which created Lake Powell, has led to the growth of Glen Canyon National Recreation Area—one of the most popular destinations in the national park system. More recently, the Wilderness Act has allowed for the designation of the Paria Canyon-Vermilion Cliffs, Ashdown Gorge, and Box-Death Hollow wilderness areas, which are administered by the Bureau of Land Management and accessible only on foot or on horseback. The proposed designation of further large tracts of land as "wilderness" (whether there is any true wilderness left is subject to healthy debate these days) continues to attract considerable controversy in southern Utah—an area with a strong tradition of land use.

The combined population of the Washington, Iron, Garfield, and Kane counties that make up southern Utah's Land of Color is now nearly 79,000 and growing rapidly. The city of St. George, home of Dixie College, the Mormon temple and tabernacle, and many fine pioneer buildings, is now a popular destination for people arriving in southern Utah via Interstate 15. The city's warm climate, relaxed living, proximity to several national and state parks, and excellent recreational opportunities and visitor facilities have made it the fastest growing city in Utah.

But St. George's expansion has required careful planning. Over the last few years, concern has grown about the fate of the desert tortoises and other endangered species living close to, or in, the city. The country's desert tortoise populations, which have diminished drastically over the past century, were recently accorded protection under the Endangered Species Act, as a result of human threats to their native habitat. Though locally viewed as an integral part of the desert landscape and a possible boon for tourism, the desert tortoises are nevertheless unknowingly part of a debate involving land development destined to continue as southern Utah moves into the 21st century.

The Geology of Southern Utah

Southern Utah's geological story may be told in two parts: the first, and longest, part is the tale of a region that lay for millions of years beneath the sea or near sea level; of clays, muds, sands, gravels, and the limey skeletons of marine creatures being deposited above each other until roughly three vertical miles of these sedimentary materials had accumulated and hardened into rock. The second part of the saga involves a great monolithic block of land being pushed up slowly from the surrounding lowlands; a series of breaks and folds appearing in the rock; and the subsequent action of streams methodically cutting their way into these rising sedimentary rocks.

AGES OF ROCK MAKING

The depth of the Grand Canyon makes it possible to see rocks here from each of the first three eras of the earth's past. The oldest strata, which were formed during the Archeozoic era, may be seen only in the canyon's dark inner gorge. They have been severely distorted by heat and pressure, making accurate interpretation of their original nature difficult. No evidence of life is found in the crumpled Archeozoic strata, and their uppermost layers are all missing. These igneous rocks are thought to be around 3.5 billion years old and to represent the eroded roots of mountains, similar in form to the modern Alps.

Above these primitive strata, in several places, sit the tilted formations of the Proterozoic era. Most of the rocks are hundreds of millions of years old. Although one of these formations is composed of igneous rock, most of the strata were deposited as sediments in and along the edge of a very early sea that covered the area, or were left behind in arid basins by large rivers. These ancient sedimentary rocks are believed to have been over 12,000 feet thick. Although they reveal no identifiable species of animals and plants, they do contain abundant indirect evidence of the probable existence of molluscs and fossils of colonial blue-green algae called stromatolites. Before the end of this era the strata were disturbed and broken by crustal movements, which tilted some rock masses from their horizontal position to create a topography similar to that of the Great Basin of today. Over millennia, erosive forces removed enormous portions of the uplifted blocks—in a few places all of them. In others, the corners of the tilted strata remain to tell the story of these ancient times.

Most of the formations seen from the rim of the Grand Canyon are the level formations of the Paleozoic era. Despite the fact that this area was near or below sea level much of the time, it experienced considerable crustal unrest, with a sea advancing and retreating several times. During the times when the sea was absent, erosion occurred. As a result, some of the strata are missing. The fossil record in the sedimentary rocks below the rim reveals abundant evidence of marine life

The areas covered in this section are primarily within the state of Utah, but the Grand Canyon and the Arizona Strip in northern Arizona have also been included. The Grand Canyon is in the same geological province as southern Utah's tablelands—an area known as the Colorado Plateau; it is, therefore, part of the same geological story. At the Grand Canyon, 12 formations representing three geological eras have been exposed by the powerful erosive action of the Colorado River and its tributaries. Here, written in the canyon's colorful strata, is the story of our planet. In 1880, When geologist Clarence E. Dutton, a member of Major John Wesley Powell's expeditions to the Grand Canyon region, made the first geological reconnaissance of the High Plateaus he wrote of the Grand Canyon:

Nature is more easily read here than elsewhere. She seems at times in these solitudes to have lifted from her countenance the veil of mystery which she habitually wears in the haunts of men. The land is stripped of its normal clothing; its cliffs and canyons have dissected and laid open its tissues and framework, and 'he who runs may read' if his eyes have been duly opened.

and some of land-dwelling animals. Before the end of that era, animals and plants emerged from the sea and made the land their home, beginning the Age of Reptiles.

Rocks of the Mesozoic era that followed are widespread in the region, though almost absent near the Grand Canyon rim. With certain exceptions, the bulk of the strata here belongs to the sedimentary formations laid down during the Triassic and Jurassic periods. These rocks make up the Chocolate Cliffs, the Vermilion Cliffs, the White Cliffs, the Grey Cliffs and the Pink Cliffs, which, together, are known as the Grand Staircase. Viewed as a staircase, the top step would be Bryce Canyon descending to the Grand Canyon at the bottom. The sediments accumulated under

Shale patterns, near Paria

A. *Primitive folded mountains with granite base.*

B. *Mountains eroded to their roots.*

A. *Land sinks and sediments accumulate.*

B. *Region uplifted and broken by faults.*

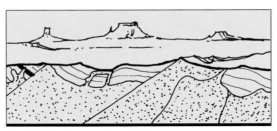

C. *Highlands are again eroded away.*

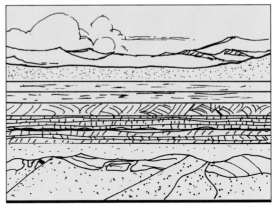

Region sinks again. Thick layers of sediments accumulate.

a variety of conditions: some were born beneath the sea; others were laid down along the edge of the water in bogs and marshes; and thick beds were deposited in deserts by the wind (see chart, page 24). In these rocks are entombed the bones of giant reptiles and other creatures. According to the fossil record, the dinosaurs, near the culmination of their reign, became monstrous in size. The last years of the Mesozoic era saw the retreat of the last of the vast inland seas from the North American continent and the extinction of the dinosaurs and other giant reptiles.

THE DINOSAURS DIE

The sediments that were deposited during the subsequent Age of Mammals, or Cenozoic era, are locally all of terrestrial origin. At the beginning of the Tertiary period, about 65 million years ago,

there was considerable crustal movement in the West. Most geologists now believe that this was caused by the movement of the Pacific Ocean continental plate sliding under the North American continental plate—a process known as subduction. This eastward movement caused the Southwest to be squeezed, gently folded, and broadly uplifted. As a consequence, what would become the great rocky rampart of the Colorado Plateau started a gradual elevation, until it was

eventually a mile above the surrounding land. This event also created the Rocky Mountains and is known as the Laramide Orogeny. Although the principal range runs south through Colorado, an important spur—the Wasatch Range—extends southward into Utah.

In some parts, where the crust bent more gently, downwarped basins developed, such as the Paradox Basin west of the Uncompahgre Uplift in eastern Utah. These depressions caught the waters from the highlands, forming freshwater lakes. The water also carried material into the lake that forms the basis of rock, including gravel, sand, volcanic fragments, silts, limes, or mixtures and combinations of the above. Naturally the mountains and highlands, which supplied these materials, became considerably worn. Even though deposits of this age are widespread, the most spectacular display is found in the 1,000-foot layer of freshwater limestone in Bryce Canyon and Cedar Breaks. Colored by oxides of iron and magnesium, these yellow, purple, pink, and white limestones make up the Pink Cliffs of the Claron

Geologic Cross Section of the Cedar Breaks – Zion – Grand Canyon Region

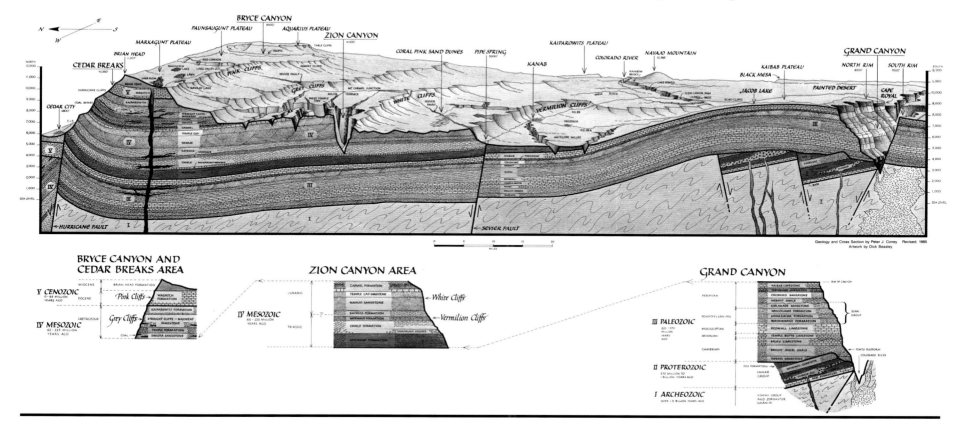

Geology and Cross Section by Peter J. Coney. Revised: 1985
Artwork by Dick Beasley

member of the Wasatch Formation, which are thought to come from a giant body of water dubbed Lake Flagstaff by geologists.

In the second half of the Cenozoic era, probably beginning in the Miocene epoch, the district became the scene of considerable volcanic activity, perhaps resulting from the relaxation of the compression associated with the Laramide Orogeny that had begun millions of years earlier. Molten lava was able to force its way up along widening faults in the crustal rocks, giving rise to thick, dark lava flows when it reached the surface. One can see ample evidence of this in parts of the

Pine Valley Mountain, the Beaver (Tushar) Mountains, at Brian Head near Cedar Breaks, and atop the Paunsagunt Plateau. Many of these early volcanic rocks have been moved from their original beds of deposition during later periods of erosion. In cases where the magma was unable to reach the surface due to the thickness of the overlying sedimentary rocks, intrusive igneous rocks, known as laccoliths, resulted. This process accounts for laccolithic mountain ranges, such as the Pine Valley, La Sal, Henry, and other mountains found in Utah, whose igneous cores were later uncovered by erosion. Later erosion, how-

ever, reduced much of this uplifted land to a well-drained, relatively level surface.

Although the freshwater limestones and volcanic debris contain snails and other interesting fossils that once lived in Lake Flagstaff, they reveal little evidence of the mammals that were rapidly evolving. Elsewhere in Utah, however, fossils of early horses and other mammals have been recovered from rocks contemporaneous with the Wasatch Formation of southern Utah.

For the most part—and the exceptions are noted—the volcanic eruptions of the Tertiary to Quaternary epochs marked the end of rock

The Five Chapters

CHAPTER	SUB-CHAPTERS	DESCRIPTION OF THE "PAGES" OR FORMATIONS	FORMATION	LOCATIONS
V **Cenozoic** 70 million years ago	*Miocene Epoch* 14 million years long. "Golden Age of Mammals." Greatest variety of mammals of all times.	Lower members white, limey and sandy beds. Upper beds grey conglomerates and volcanic breccias, sometimes with ash, tuff and chalcedony. Occaisionally capped with younger lavas.	*Brian Head*	Brian Head Paunsagunt Plateau
	Eocene Epoch 20 million years long. Modern mammals present. Small, dog-size horses with five-toes present.	White, purple, yellow, but mostly pink limestones, some with conglomerates and siltstones. Deposited by streams & in lakes. Colors due to small amounts of iron and manganese oxides.	*Wasatch*	Bryce Canyon Cedar Breaks Table Cliffs
IV **Mesozoic** 155 million years ago	*Cretaceous Period* 65 million years long. Reptiles at zenith. Largest forms and toothed birds became extinct. Modern snakes, birds, insects and flowering plants developed. Few primitive mammals. Last great epicontinental sea came over the land and retreated. The Rocky Mountains were born near the close of the period.	Dark grey and yellow-brown sandstones cemented by lime. Deposited in irregular beds by streams. Contains many fossils.	*Kaiparowits*	Paria Valley below Bryce Canyon
		Creamy yellow-brown sandstones alternating with grey to green-brown shale and sandy shale. Deposited in seas and lagoons.	*Wahweap*	Coal Creek Canyon Long Valley Paria Valley
		Massive beds of light yellow to buff sandstones deposited in in seas and lagoons. A cliff maker. Contains coal and abundant fossils.	*Straight Cliffs*	Paria Valley
		Dark, drab shales. Highly fossiliferous with beds of coal. Deposited in marshes and beneath sea.	*Tropic*	
		Brown and buff sandstones and conglomerates. Loosely cemented stream deposits. Some fossil wood.	*Dakota*	Mount Carmel Grosvenor's Arch Kodachrome Flat Mount Carmel
	Jurassic Period 45 million years long. Reptiles the dominant form of life on land, sea and air. The first toothed birds found in rocks of this age. First mammals and modern conifer trees developed. Desert environment followed by a marine invasion from the north.	Yellow and red sandstones and some fine conglomerates. Is an approximate equivalent of the famous Morrison formation.	*Winsor*	Meadow Gulch
		Rough-bedded marine sandstone, limestone, and white gypsum.	*Curtis*	Cannonville
		Massive, deep red sandstones, sometimes with yellow, white or cream bands. Thickens eastward.	*Entrada*	Caps Zion Temples Dameron Valley
		Resistant deposits of grey marine limestone, sandstone & shale turn to brilliant red sandstone east of Cockscomb. Many fossils.	*Carmel*	Glen Canyon region
	Boundary line between Jurassic and Triassic periods is indistinct locally	Massive cliffs of crossbedded (windblown) sandstone weakly cemented by lime & iron oxides. Color may be red, white, or with red base and white top and irregular interfingerings of the two colors. Contains layers of dolomite and clay. In some regions, contains intrusions of Kayenta formation. Few fossils. Deposition probably began in Triassic and continued into Jurassic.	*Navajo*	Zion National Park Glen Canyon Snow Canyon State Park Cockscomb Cutoff
	Triassic Period 45 million years long. Reptiles the dominant form of life on land, sea and air. The first toothed birds found in rocks of this age. First mammals and modern conifer trees developed. Desert environment followed by a marine invasion from the north.	Layers of maroon sandstone and color-banded siltstone. Forms a springline. Contains dinosaur tracks of Triassic period.	*Kayenta*	Zion National Park St. George
		Top layer a massive cliff-making white or crimson sandstone. Is underlain by red sandstone and shale. Continental beds.	*Moenave*	Kanab Silver Reef
		Colorful beds of volcanic ash, oozes and silts. Stream deposits in fresh water. Contains fossil wood and minerals.	*Chinle*	Paria Townsite Zion National Park
		Grey to white coarse sandstone and conglomerate. Usually forms a cliff. Stream deposits on eroded surface. Much petrified wood.	*Shinarump*	Hurricane Mesa Rockville
		Red-brown shales and sandstones with white gypsum and blue limestone. Deposited in sea, along flood plains and by streams.	*Moenkopi*	Fredonia Virgin Anticline
III **Paleozoic** 375 million years ago	*Permian Period* 45 million years long. Amophibians were dominant animals. Cycads and conifers were present for the first time. The early Permian climate locally was arid, but near the end the sea advanced over the land and then retreated. In the east at the close of this period, the Appalachian mountains were formed.	Massive, resistant fossiliferous sandy limestones. Shallow sea deposits. Often contains much chert.	*Kaibab*	Hurricane Cliffs rim of Grand Canyon
		Red sandstones and shales. Some gypsum and limestone.	*Toroweap*	Grand Canyon
		Light buff wind-blown sandstone. A cliff-maker.	*Coconino*	
		Blood red and bright red shales and silts, with some thin sandstone and limestone. Deposited in pools. Many fossils.	*Hermit Shale*	
		Mostly blood red with some grey sandstones. The top members are resistant, forming cliffs. Deposited by the sea or on flood plains by rivers. Contains amphibian tracks and fossil ferns.	*Supai*	
	Mississippian Period 25 million years long. Ancient sharks. Fossil Ferns.	Almost pure blue-grey limestone ledge, superficially colored by the two formations above. Contains plant and animal skeletons.	*Redwall*	
	Devonian Period Early fish, simple ferns.	Pale purple sandy shale and limestone. Found in troughs in Muav.	*Temple Butte*	
	Cambrian Period 100 million years. First age of abundant fossils. Sea animals and plants. Most rocks marine.	Buff to grey limestone, sandstone and cliff-making dolomite.	*Muav*	
		Buff to gree-grey shales and sandstones. Shallow sea deposits.	*Bright Angel*	
		Brown sandstone cliff.	*Tapeats*	
II **Proterozoic**	600 million years long. Fossils are scarce but there is evidence of algae, sponges and wormlike creatures. Deposits were subsequently tilted and much worn.	Unkar "wedge series." Dox: red and grey sandstones and shales; Shinumo: resistant purple quartzite; Hakatai: arid basin deposit of deep red shales and sandstones; Diabase: Igneous layer; Bass: blue-grey marine limestone; Hotuata: a conglomerate.	*Dox/Shinumo/ Hakatai/ Diabase/Bass/ Hotuata*	
I **Archeozoic**	A billion years or longer. Evidence of life indirect. Universally rocks of this age present an eroded surface.	Strongly folded schist and gneiss from rocks distorted in a great mountain building movement. Original beds probably igneous and sedimentary. The eroded bases of these ancient mountains are intruded by masses and streaks of pink to grey granite.	*Vishnu Schists*	

making in this region. For over a billion years sediments had been accumulating above each other, until approximately 15,000 feet of geological strata were represented.

EROSION

As this region was elevated, it was subjected to distortion and fracturing in the rock. In a few sections the crust has been folded, as in the Kanarra Fold found in Zion National Park's Kolob Canyons Unit. In other areas the strata have been broken, and one part has been thrust high above the opposite member along fractures known as faults. As the folds have varied from gentle bends to broad upwarps, measured in miles, so too have the breaks ranged from small cracks to long fractures with several thousands of feet of vertical displacement. The greatest breaks are those that run roughly north and south, parallel to each other along the east and west sides of the high plateaus (see the geological cross section diagram on the previous page). These faults developed approximately 15 million years ago, 50 million years after the beginning of the Laramide Orogeny. The greatest vertical movement occurred along the magnificent Hurricane Fault, which extends southward from Cedar City to beyond the Grand Canyon. Interstate 15 runs alongside this fracture to Anderson's Junction. The second break, the Sevier Fault, parallels Highway 89 south from Panguitch to the Mount Carmel Junction and continues for some distance beyond Pipe Spring. You can see the third fault, the Paunsagunt, from the rim of Bryce Canyon.

Of the several broad and lofty platforms that have been uplifted east of the faults, the westernmost is the Markagunt (*mar-kah'-gunt* is a Paiute word meaning "highland of trees"). The Markagunt Plateau lies east of the Hurricane Fault, tilts a few degrees toward the east, and reaches as high as 11,315 feet in places. Near Highway 89 it abuts the Sevier Fault and a second plateau, the Paunsagunt (*paun-sawgunt*, Paiute for "home of the beaver"). From the eastern edge of the level-topped Paunsagunt, one may observe the even crestline of the Aquarius Plateau (Aquarius is a Latin word meaning "water bearer"), a splendid, once-glaciated platform 11,000 feet above the sea. (See diagram on page 23 for relationship of faults.)

Farther south, in the upwarped Grand Canyon region, these faults continue. Here, as a result of earlier upwarping, erosion has been able to reduce the thickness of the sedimentary layers to a greater degree than in the Utah section. In most places, younger rocks have been eroded away, except for a few outliers of the older Chocolate Cliffs of the Moenkopi Formation. To the south, in Arizona, are four other plateaus: the Shivwits (*Sheev'-wits* refers to a clan of Paiutes), the Uinkaret (*you-in-karet*, a Paiute word meaning "place where the pines grow"), the Kanab (*kaynab*, a Paiute word meaning "willow"), and the Kaibab (*ky-bab*, a Paiute word meaning "mountain lying down"). The four are collectively known as the Coconino Plateau, from the Havasupai Indian word *co-co-ne-no* meaning "little water." Into this great "blister," the Colorado River has downcut a deep path, which, along with the action of its tributaries and erosion, has led to the vast gash known as the Grand Canyon.

The streams that flowed over this region before the Colorado Plateau began to rise were gentle and meandering. The elevation of the land beneath them changed the gradient, giving the streams new energy and enabling them to downcut tortuous channels in the slowly rising strata. Stream-cut, narrow canyons began to

appear, and prodigious quantities of worn rock were carried away by the streams to the sea. Many of these streams are tiny much of the year, often becoming completely dry. But since this arid land offers little in the way of vegetation to hold the water in check, disastrous flash floods are common during the rainy season. It is the scouring action of swollen, silt-laden streams that has created the labyrinthian canyon system in this area, along with a number of other rock formations, such as natural bridges.

The broken edges of the elevated blocks and the freshly cut canyon walls have been excellent targets for all agents of erosion. The rain has mercilessly and persistently vented its wrath on these naked ledges, and, aided by wind, by frost, and by the roots of plants searching for a foothold, has forced the walls to crumble and recede. Strata that were soft and poorly consolidated have been readily worn away, but where they have proved more resistant tablelands, or plateaus, have resulted. In the Grand Canyon benches have formed. In southern Utah, these stubborn strata break off to the south as the Grand Staircase, descending from the refreshing coolness of the higher terraces to the splendor of the desert below. The land has thus been torn away in great layers, revealing, with each step downward, areas of the earth's crust of increasing age. At the Grand Canyon the amount of erosion, both above and below the rim, seems almost incredible.

ICE AND FIRE ROCKS

The last Ice Age, in Pleistocene times, also left its mark here. There is ample evidence of local glaciation on the Aquarius, Tushar, and Markagunt plateaus. West of the highlands, a large intercontinental lake accumulated, which eventually devel-

oped an outlet in southern Idaho and drained via the Portneuf, Snake, and Columbia rivers into the Pacific Ocean. At one time this lake, known as Lake Bonneville, filled much of what is now called the Great Basin. This great geological province is located in western Utah and eastern Nevada, just north of southern Utah's Land of Color. A large section of the Great Basin, which includes Wheeler Peak, has been protected since 1980 as Great Basin National Park. Lake Bonneville was about 350 miles long, 145 miles wide, and reached a depth of 1,050 feet. Salt Lake City's Great Salt Lake is a remnant of this massive body of water.

Examples of recent Quaternary-era "fire rocks" may be seen along the roadside in many places in this region. Eroded sediments of almost every age have been capped with lava in one place or another. Although this basaltic rock usually was poured out onto the surface from fissures in the earth's crust, eruptive rocks may be found in the dead cones near Hurricane, in Snow Canyon State Park's Dammeron Valley, on the Uinkaret Plateau in Arizona, and in many other places.

Today, the high plateaus of southern Utah's Land of Color are undoubtedly its most distinctive feature. Their edges have been shattered by rain and wind to create the intricate castellations and geomorphs found at Bryce Canyon and Cedar Breaks. Their heartlands have been deeply incised by tempestuous streams that, as at Zion, have carved deep, straight-walled chasms. And the most remarkable of all these chasms is located at the southernmost "step" of the Grand Staircase, where the relentless scouring action of the Colorado River has created the incomparable abyss of the Grand Canyon. Touched in high places by glaciers, these silent plateaus are majestic reminders of the fascinating geological story this landscape has to tell.

All living creatures have a few fundamental needs that must be satisfied if they are to stay alive. These essentials are air (oxygen), water, favorable temperature, food, and shelter.

In this diverse world of ours, these necessities are unevenly distributed; in some places water is abundant, but the temperature is low; in others, food is scarce; in still others water is a rare commodity. Consequently, in order for plants and animals to inhabit these widely differing sites, they have had to develop structures or take on functions that enable them to cope with the things they lack locally. For example, plants faced with a shortage of water, such as desert cactus, may solve their problems by developing a waxy coating over the leaf and stem to prevent evaporation; they may produce a widespread but shallow root system to capture every bit of available moisture during infrequent rains; they may send tap roots deep into the ground to secure water from underground sources; or they may modify their leaves into spines, which not only prevents water loss through a reduction in the leaf surface but also deters animals from tearing them apart for food.

Animal adaptations are also varied. Some creatures, such as bears, living in regions where they experience prolonged periods of cold, resort to hibernation during the winter months. Desert dwellers often solve the problem of heat and avoid the dangers of water loss by foraging only at night. Reptiles, like the Mojave Desert's slow-moving desert tortoise, avoid

extreme heat and cold by becoming dormant in burrows. Those creatures that live in places where food is available only during a few months or weeks frequently provide for the balance of the year by constructing storage chambers, which they fill during the short, but busy, harvest time.

As a result of these many adaptations, few areas remain devoid of living things; desert dwellers thrive in the arid heat; subalpine inhabitants successfully cope with the problems of cold and short growing seasons; and between these two extremes a multitude of creatures exist, each living within the niche to which it has become adjusted.

MERRIAM'S LIFE ZONES

In 1894, C. Hart Merriam, who had studied plant and animal associations in the Rocky Mountains and the Grand Canyon region, decided that North America contained seven large and distinctive biotic communities, which he named "life zones." Not only did he identify and describe each but he also postulated that they existed because of two factors: the adjustment the creatures within the zones had made to the total quantity of heat during the season of growth and reproduction and the mean temperature of a brief period covering the hottest part of the year. Subsequent studies have shown that the causes are not nearly as simple as that. On the contrary, the animal plant community is affected by a

complex combination of factors, such as the amount of available moisture, kind of soil, exposure to sunlight, wind direction and velocity, competition, and so on.

In southern Utah's Land of Color, where elevations vary between 2,800 feet and 11,000 feet, one may drive through as many as five of these life zones, most of them separated from their neighbors by interesting zones of transition containing some plants and animals from more than one zone. The life zones can be separated arbitrarily on the basis of elevation, but since the change in vegetation on the north slope of a mountain may be as much as 1,000 feet lower than the south side, this is not a reliable guide. In Zion Canyon, for example, where towering cliffs cast long shadows on one side of the canyon, plants that should be as much as 3,000 feet above their across-canyon neighbors are found growing at the

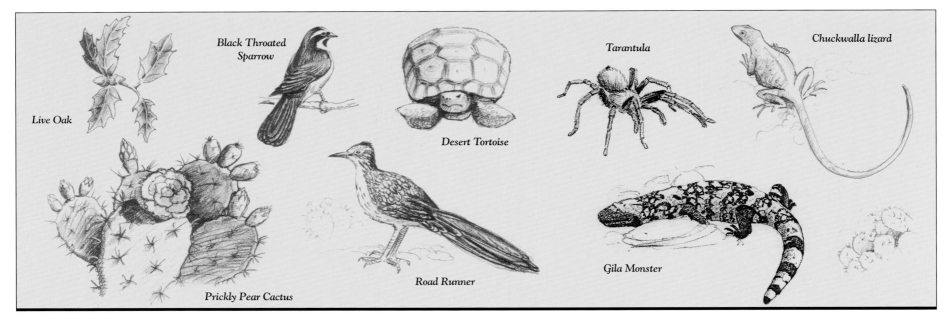

Lower Sonoran Zone

same elevation, less than a hundred yards away!

The following description has been written to enable visitors to understand and enjoy these diverse life zones while visiting the Southwest. Even though some plants, such as the dandelion, grow at all elevations, plants are generally the best guide in determining life zones. Since birds and animals are usually quite adaptable, the following species may be encountered at almost any elevation: badger, pocket gopher, white-footed mouse, wood rat, mule deer, coyote, porcupine, and bobcat. Although the shy, rarely seen mountain lion, or cougar, lives in the higher mountains and is found throughout Zion National Park's 3,666-to 8,726-foot elevations, it is known to cross the deserts as it moves from range to range, hunting deer and small game.

The list of plants and animals found, and noted, in each zone described below is far from complete. Rather, only a few distinctive representatives have been included.

LOWER SONORAN ZONE

Elevations to 4,000 feet

The indicator plant here, often found in association with the valuable honey mesquite, screw bean, and desert barberry, is the deep green, many-stemmed creosote bush, known in the West as "chaparral." Black brush and live oak (holly oak) grow at the upper limits and connect with the zone above. From April until midsummer the bloom of an impressive variety of cacti decorates the desert landscape.

Reptiles, which are unable to regulate their body temperatures physiologically, abound in this habitat. Several, such as the gila monster and chuckwalla lizard, live in this zone only. Others, like the colorful red racer and western king snake, may move into the lower parts of the Upper Sonoran Zone. Small subpopulations of the unique Mojave Desert tortoise are found at Beaver Dam and in the red rock/dune areas north of St. George, and there are also tortoises living in the Hurricane area, descended from introduced tortoise species. After millions of years of existence, native desert tortoise populations in the Mojave and Sonoran deserts have declined rapidly over the last century, as a result of direct and indirect encroachment on their habitat by Man. In 1989, the desert tortoise was given protection under the Endangered Species Act for a number of reasons, of which the most important is the spread of an exotic, deadly upper respiratory disease that is wiping out many desert tortoises. Visitors are reminded that they may observe these protected creatures but that they may not touch them. For more information about where to view desert tortoises, contact the Bureau of Land Management in St. George.

Easily identified by the white tail it carries over its back, an interesting little mammal known as the antelope ground squirrel can be seen in the Lower Sonoran Zone during any season. It can be found searching for food in the middle of the day when most animals have sought shade. The kangaroo rat, which lives in both the Lower and Upper Sonoran zones, feeds only at night, holing up in its burrow during the daytime. It may sometimes be seen in the glare of a car's head-lights as it scurries awkwardly across the highways during its nocturnal foraging.

Of the several birds found in this environment, none is more unusual and more readily identified with the Southwest than the road-runner, a lizard-eating bird with a jack-handle tail, which may be seen rushing along the road on long, inelegant legs. The grey, black-and-white-marked loggerhead shrike, the black-throated sparrow, the house finch, the mockingbird, the phainopepla, the vermilion flycatcher, and the Gambel's quail are also confined largely to this zone.

The Virgin River provides a pleasant riparian environment for desert life at this elevation and offers a verdant counterpoint to the desert's subtle shades. At water's edge, desert plants abruptly give way to thick stands of the broad-leafed Fremont cottonwood, and willow, as well as the exotic pink-flowered tamerisk tree, which once it has taken hold dominates its neighbors by creating an overly salty environment in which they are unable to thrive—a common sight throughout the

Upper Sonoran Zone

Southwest. The muskrat abounds in the nearby swamps. The river is also a popular venue for the American coot, the marsh wren, the common yellowthroat, the black Phoebe, and other birds that find tasty insects swarming over its surface, or in vegetation along its banks.

Most of the settlements in Utah's Dixie are located in this Lower Sonoran Zone.

UPPER SONORAN ZONE

4,000 feet to 6,800 feet

The grey-green, pungent sagebrush is frequently the dominant shrub in this life zone, although it may be found in association with shadscale, or more frequently, rabbitbrush, whose yellow flowers brighten roadsides in the fall. Piñon pine and juniper trees, found together in the Southwest

so often that this zone is called the piñon-juniper zone, grow in thick, dwarf stands in many places. Two species of piñon grow here, one of which is the unusual single leaf piñon. Two kinds of juniper trees also make their home here, with the Rocky Mountain juniper found near the upper reaches of the zone and the Utah juniper near its base. Local residents call the junipers "cedar trees," and this erroneous name, originally given by early pioneers, led to the naming of Cedar Breaks National Monument. During the summer, a colorful array of wildflowers, such as Palmer penstemon, scarlet gilia, and sacred datura bloom abundantly by the side of the road. The creamy trumpet-flowered sacred datura is also known as Zion lily and is an emblematic flower in the area.

Some snakes and lizards from the Lower Sonoran Zone also live here, but except for the short-horned toad (lizard) and the western rattle-snake, few extend into the upper limits of the zone. Although there is no mammal that does not descend into the Lower Sonoran from this area, the desert jackrabbit, the cottontail rabbit, or grey rock squirrel do not go much higher on the mountains and plateaus than this.

The sage sparrow, the sage grouse, the lark sparrow, and the Brewer's sparrow all live in the shrubby area while the pinyon jay, the black-throated grey warbler, and the bush tit make the piñon-juniper forest their home.

Most communities in southern Utah, outside the Dixie area, are in this life zone.

TRANSITION ZONE

6,800 to 8,000 feet

Gambel oak and the important, timber-producing western yellow pine (more popularly known as ponderosa pine) are excellent markers of this zone. At its upper limits Douglas fir and white fir flourish. At lower elevations antelope brush, serviceberry, tall sage, and manzanita grow profusely, although the latter is found in association with yellow pine. Along the streams the narrow-leaf cottonwood, the red-barked birch, and the chokecherry take root. During the summer, bluebells, geraniums, and globemallow adorn the landscape.

The wandering garter snake is common along the stream courses where, in the lower parts of the zone, one may also encounter the western rattlesnake. Although no mammal is confined to this region alone, many species listed in the sub-alpine Canadian Zone above also live here. Several species of warbler nest here along with the dark-eyed junco, the western bluebird, and the lovely mountain bluebird.

Transition Zone

Because the Transition Zone blends into the others so gradually, it is impossible to draw exact lines to mark where it begins. North of Glendale in Long Valley, this zone may be found along Highway 89 in the upper half of the canyon. Its markers persist along the highway almost to Hatch, although a few Upper Sonoran plants mingle with them, particularly on the sunlit slopes. Much of Red Canyon and the lower regions of Bryce Canyon National Park are in this zone. It is also found along the eastern approach to Cedar Breaks National Monument, via Highway 14, as far as the Duck Creek area, where it gradually gives way to the Canadian Zone. In Coal Creek Canyon, between Cedar City and Cedar Breaks, the zone is not conspicuous, probably due to the convoluted geology of the area; at the elevation where it should begin the canyon,

which is cut through the Straight Cliffs Formation, narrows considerably, with the consequent long shadows favoring the growth of plants in the Canadian Zone.

CANADIAN ZONE

8,000 feet to 9,500 feet

The golden aspen with its soft silvery bark and shimmering light green leaves, set against a backdrop of symmetrical, deep green-blue spruce and Douglas fir, makes this region one of the most pleasant of all those encountered in southern Utah's Land of Color. Associated shrubs include the snowberry and chokecherry. Limber pine may be found in a few places.

The energetic Fremont chickaree, or tree squirrel, the inquisitive chipmunk, and its larger

*Douglas
Fir*

*Prairie
Dog*

Mountain Snowberry

Canadian Zone

Bristlecone Pine

Mule Deer

Hudsonian Zone

relative, the golden-mantled ground squirrel, use the products of the forest to increase their winter larder. Prairie dogs build their towns in open meadows here, but are found at lower elevations, too. Marmots are often seen along the meadow's edge, in the rocks, or in slab piles left from saw mills. The hairy woodpecker and the hermit thrush are native birds that may be seen at this elevation.

The Canadian Zone may be found on both approaches to Cedar Breaks and on the Rainbow Point road in Bryce Canyon National Park.

HUDSONIAN ZONE

9,500 feet to 11,000 feet

Two trees are most representative of this topmost zone: Englemann spruce and subalpine fir. Although they both extend well into the Canadian Zone, where they grow in association with Douglas fir, white fir, and blue spruce, only these two storm-loving evergreens are able to endure the rugged environment on the hills and in the valleys of the colder Hudsonian Zone. Near the edges of the cliffs, and on the promontories, ancient bristlecone pine (thought to be the oldest living trees in the world) and limber pine replace or join them. Aspen extends into the lower parts of this habitat.

During the summer tourist season, the meadows here are decorated with a lavish display of bluebells, delphinium, Indian paintbrush, penstemon, and wallflowers. Beneath the regal evergreens the large white-and-blue-spurred columbines form an enchanting carpet, while in wet places death camas, monkshood, and marsh marigold bloom. Visitors to Cedar Breaks will be rewarded by a glorious show of color at this time of year.

The golden-mantled ground squirrel, the Fremont chickaree, and the marmot also live at this elevation. Deer that summer here are sleek and fat. Three-toed woodpeckers, gray jays, and Clark's nutcrackers do not descend very far from these high altitudes.

At Brian Head, north of Cedar Breaks, where the uppermost limits of this zone are reached and perhaps slightly exceeded, exposure to the cold winds has dwarfed the trees. Glowing phlox fills the air with fragrance in July, and the less pleasantly perfumed alpine primrose blooms beneath the summit a bit later in the season. The rock rabbit, or pika, is the only inhabitant of this rocky environment.

Hints on Photographing Southern Utah

For many people, words alone cannot capture southern Utah's thrilling desert scenery. As a result, increasing numbers of visitors are turning to photography in an attempt to record this remarkable landscape. Photographers unfamiliar with the region, however, may easily overlook some fine shots. By drawing on the collective knowledge and experience of park naturalists, park rangers, and professional photographers, we have prepared the following suggestions. We hope that the experiences of these experts will help you in obtaining good photographs of the area.

EXPOSURE

A combination of factors, including the high altitude, the clean, dry air, the scarcity of vegetation, and the light colors of most rocks, generally requires shortening of the average time of exposure. If this is not done, the resulting over-exposures will "wash out" many dramatic colors.

With exceptions as noted, the following suggestions have been made for photographs of scenery under normal lighting conditions. If taking pictures in early morning hours or late in the afternoon, the exposures will require a longer time than those recommended, as will pictures taken in the shade, beneath clouds, and so on. When in doubt, or when the picture simply *must* be right, take three exposures, one "right on," one a half-stop "over," and one a half-stop "under."

If a light meter is used, it may give a surprisingly high reading. The light meter is dependable, though, if one is careful not to get too much sky in the readings and, conversely, in the morning and afternoon, deep shadows in the foreground are not allowed to figure too importantly.

Since little adjustment can be made on automatic cameras, pay attention to the time of day in order to obtain the best results.

TIME OF DAY

Although some photography guides suggest that midday shots (10 A.M. to 2 P.M.) are best, this advice is not appropriate in southern Utah. The early morning hours offer one of the best times to shoot, with afternoon shots frequently turning out even better, as clouds roll in affording more dramatic light. Evening shots are often quite beautiful. Southern Utah's famous red cliffs photograph especially well at sunset.

CONTRAST

One of the singular things about a southwestern landscape is the contrast between the colors of the cliffs and pinnacles and the blue of the sky, the whiteness of a cloud, or the verdant greens of the vegetation. If the camera is set for a distance of 25 feet, objects in the foreground as close as 12 feet away are brought into sharp focus. A green branch or shrub in one corner of the photograph not only provides good contrast but also helps give depth to the shot. Colorfully clothed people also provide excellent foreground material. Choice of clothing color is important yellows and yellow-reds will "advance" in photographs; greens and browns will remain neutral; and blues and blue-greens will "retreat."

FILTERS

A polarizing filter, although effective for red cliffs and autumn colors, and useful for providing variety, can easily be overused. Open the aperture one full stop above the indicated meter readings when using such a filter.

The skylight filter is helpful on distant shots and, because it requires no extra exposure, can be

Watchman at Sunset, Zion National Park

Timbertop Mountain and Nagunt Mesa, Finger Canyons of the Kolob

used almost universally. A clean skylight filter provides good protection for an expensive lens.

The Type A filter can be used with daylight film to produce lovely sunsets. Look through it first to see the effect. Sunsets can be shot successfully immediately after the sun goes down and for a few minutes thereafter. Although these exposures are tricky, good results can often be obtained. To make sure, take several different exposures.

LOCATION

Places offering excellent photographic possibilities in southern Utah's Land of Color are almost too numerous to mention. While many of them are directly along the highway, others are off the "beaten path." We know that it will be impossible to list them all, or to make certain that a particu-

lar location is the best choice. Nevertheless, long experience has shown that there are certain subjects of unusual interest or of proven merit with which an outsider may not be familiar. Where road directions are necessary the distances have been logged, the mileages noted, and the necessary instructions included in the descriptions that follow.

The Parowan Gap

Even though there are no special scenic highlights here, visitors interested in Indian petroglyphs (incised rock art) will find this spot a good place to photograph. One set of these "writings" is reputed to be among the few in the West that tell a story, in this case the tale of an aboriginal journey. Since the rock art has a fine southern exposure, it can be shot during most of the day, except late afternoon when some petroglyphs will be in shadow.

The rock art is located in the far end of the gap in the low range of hills 11.8 miles northwest of Parowan. To reach the site, follow Highway 127 to the outskirts of town, turning right at the first intersection. Then turn left about 2.5 miles from the point of departure at a second intersection. Follow the unpaved road past the southwest end of the Little Salt Lake and enter the gap. The road crosses a large meadow until it reaches the low hills where the Indians chipped their petroglyphs.

The Vermilion Castles in Parowan Canyon

Although satisfactory pictures may be taken here all day long, the most interesting figures are illuminated best by the afternoon sun. These

Vermilion Castles belong to the Wasatch Formation, the same beds of limestone that form the myriad sculptured forms at Bryce Canyon and Cedar Breaks.

The U.S. Forest Service provides excellent picnicking and camping facilities here. To get to this spot, turn east at the bank and library corner in Parowan, follow Highway 143 for 3.7 miles, and then turn left. The paved surface extends to the forest camp, 1.4 miles up this side canyon.

The Finger Canyons of the Kolob Terrace

Splendid afternoon pictures of these lofty red ledges may be obtained by taking the New Harmony exit from Interstate 15 and driving about three miles.

The Peninsulas of the Kolob Terrace

These formations may be photographed easily from the 5.2-mile-long paved road leading into the Kolob Unit from Interstate 15. Another very satisfying way to view them at closehand is to hike along the Taylor Creek Trail from the trailhead. Afternoon photographs are best here; the last half-hour of sunlight brings out the brilliant red coloring in the rocks.

The Vermilion Cliffs

It is most difficult to provide photographic clues for Utah's Dixieland. One is literally surrounded by ledges of chocolate, vermilion, pink, and lavender hues, making this area a joy for those people who love vivid colors. Nevertheless, this southern exposure of the Vermilion Cliffs is unusual enough to warrant special consideration.

These cliffs may be successfully photographed at any time of day, but they are particularly brilliant in the early morning or late afternoon. Many good vantage points are located west of Santa Clara, north of old Highway 91.

Classical Buildings in St. George

The beautiful white temple and the classical red tabernacle provide photographers with excellent subject matter during the morning hours. While one can hardly shoot the temple without a frame, it may be difficult to locate suitable foreground material for a picture of the tabernacle. If the camera lens has a wide enough angle, the tree across the street southeast of the building may be used.

Snow Canyon State Park

Snow Canyon may first be seen about 7.2 miles northwest of St. George, on Highway 18. A better overview is available by taking the first road on the left just beyond this point and driving to the rim on the .3-mile-long unsurfaced road. Photographs taken at the rim are best in the morning hours.

After returning to Highway 18, drive north one mile and turn left into Snow Canyon (if you stay on Highway 18 as far as the Dammeron Valley section, 3.5 miles up the road, you will find some symmetrical volcanic cinder cones, which can be photographed all day long). Excellent photographs of Snow Canyon can be taken by climbing to the top of the hills just west of the road. A hike clear across the canyon to the west wall also offers good subject matter. Easier afternoon shots can be made from the canyon floor and in the vicinity of the south campground

which, incidentally, was the site of the movies *Four Queens and a King* and *The Electric Horseman*.

Virgin Anticline

This beautiful upfold can be photographed in the morning from the east on Highway 9, and in the afternoon from the west on Highway 9 or Interstate 15.

Hurricane Mesa

On the plateau above the Hurricane Fault and west of Virgin City, a flat-topped mesa projects southward toward the highway. These multicolored cliffs can be photographed all day long since the road passes their eastern and western faces at such an angle as to afford a splendid view.

The Road to Kolob Terrace

The Scenic Backroad leading to the Kolob Terrace from Virgin City provides a number of interesting photographic possibilities. Much of the road is paved, but as it reaches the high country close to Kolob Reservoir, it changes to graded road. This route is closed by winter snow, and even rain may render it impassable or dangerous. Check road conditions with either of the two Zion National Park Visitor Centers or in Virgin City before setting off.

Vista Supreme

Near the east end of Rockville a Scenic Backroad turns south at right angles to Highway 9, crosses a bridge with its superstructure above the roadbed, and continues southward toward Smithsonian Butte. Since it climbs almost 700 feet in one mile,

Hackberry Wash, Snow Canyon State Park

its traverse by automobile requires the use of low gear. In wet weather it is slick and should be avoided. Despite these disadvantages, however, the views of Zion Canyon from this elevated position are among the best to be found, particularly in the afternoon. A turn to the right leads to the well-known ghost town of Grafton and its historic cemetery.

The Sevier Fault

Good photographs can be taken from Highway 9, about a mile west of its junction with U.S. 89.

Diana's Throne

This southernmost promontory of the White Cliffs may be photographed with good results either during the morning or afternoon, but morning shots are probably the most pleasing.

Pink Cliffs, Bryce Canyon National Park

Kanab Canyon

Good photographs of the walls of Kanab Canyon and its tributary through which the road runs can be obtained all day. Artists using these canyons as subject matter have painted landscapes of real beauty. Early morning and late afternoon shots are the most dramatic.

Red Canyon

This canyon is so beautiful that many of the uninitiated mistake it for Bryce Canyon. Since it runs east to west, the multitude of formations can be photographed from one side or the other in the morning or afternoon. Many scenic viewpoints allow motorists to pull over and take photographs in safety.

The Road to the Paria Valley Communities

You will note on the map that a section of the road to the towns southeast of Bryce Canyon traverses part of the park. Naturally, there are many beautiful viewpoints along this paved road, but these are not confined to the park alone; rather they may be encountered all along the way. The best shots here are a matter of choice. Those visitors interested in capturing the geology should drive 3.5 miles north of Tropic and 4.3 miles south of the junction of highways 12 and 54, where the road crosses the Paunsagunt Fault. To the north, the abrupt change in color from the pink Eocene deposits of the Wasatch Formation to the grey Cretaceous beds of the Wahweap-Straight Cliffs formations makes the exact fault line clearly evident. Good pictures may be had all day long.

The Floor of Bryce Canyon

The fantastic formations on the floor of this delicate amphitheater may be photographed without hiking down the trails. But the old saying "the longest way round is the sweetest way home" applies here. Photographers will first have to drive to the little village of Tropic in the Paria Valley below. At Tropic, drive to the western edge of the town and drive south (left) a half block, and then continue west again. The wide, improved road to the park boundary is 3.3 miles long. Since the road beyond the locked gate is a restricted fire road, it is necessary to walk the rest of the way into the canyon. A half-hour hike along the reasonably good trail, however, penetrates the park far enough to allow photographers to obtain splendid pictures at any time of day.

Alternatively, hikers may avoid the return ascent from the canyon by hiking down and being met by car by a member of the group at the gate in the Paria Valley.

Scenic Gems on the Cottonwood Cutoff

This new backdoor to Bryce Canyon is an unpaved road that not only provides a short cut of approximately 70 miles to the Glen Canyon National Recreation Area, but also a pathway through vivid and unusual scenery. Because of the hazards in wet weather, it is imperative that newcomers inquire about road conditions at Bryce Canyon Visitor Center before setting out. This road must always be driven with caution and at a reasonable speed, since there are some unusually steep gradients and a number of very sharp turns. But for the backroads tourist wishing to see and photograph the unusual, it has much to recommend it. The road leaves Highway 54 in Cannonville and intersects Highway 89 10.2 miles east of Glen Canyon City, Utah. It is 46.3 miles long and is paved until it reaches Kodachrome Basin State Park.

Kodachrome Basin State Park

Local residents, to whom superlative scenery is commonplace, call this region "Thorley's Pasture." A color-conscious party of explorers, representing the National Geographic Society, named it Kodachrome Flat in the 1940s. The unusual spires can be photographed at any time of day, although early morning and evening pictures

Sand Pipe at sunset, Kodachrome Basin State Park

are best. The road crosses a peninsula at a steep grade known as Shepherd Hill 5.3 miles south of the Cannonville junction. An unusual geological unconformity, perhaps an earthquake crack, is visible on the east side of the peninsula. It may be photographed during the morning hours by stopping at the bottom of the grade.

Grosvenor Arch

This natural double arch is photographed best in the afternoon. It was named for the president of the National Geographic Society by the same group that named Kodachrome Flat.

The Cottonwood Colorama

It is nearly a half mile across this arena of almost unbelievable color at the north end of Cotton-wood Canyon. It may be photographed well from the south; however, those people entering from the northern route will probably find it best to sign the register at the north end and take photographs while driving south.

Glen Canyon Dam

Excellent photographs of the dam can be taken around midday from the walk on the Glen Canyon bridge, or from either of the viewpoints provided by the Bureau of Reclamation on both sides of the canyon. More skill will be needed for shots taken when the gorge is in part shadow.

The Old Paria Townsite

The road to this ghost town leaves Highway 89 between Kanab and Glen Canyon near the 34-mile marker at the northernmost point on this

Grosvenor Arch

highway. The six-mile-long, unsurfaced road should not be traveled in wet weather, and then with caution. Some walls may be photographed successfully all day. The set constructed for the movie *Sargents Three* adds interest.

Ship Rock

A few miles west of Fredonia and north of the road to Pipe Spring National Monument stands an outlier of the chocolate cliffs, strongly suggestive of a ship. Though it may be necessary to walk a few hundred yards, beautiful photographs can be taken here in the afternoon.

Pipe Spring National Monument

Pipe Spring can be photographed during the morning or afternoon, although morning shots are best. Since the associated buildings are on both sides of the fort, they too make good material for photographs all day.

Strawberry Point

Strawberry Point, reached by driving nine miles south from Highway 14 just after the highway

crosses Asay Creek, is a jewel and well worth a trip to photograph it. Good photographs of the vista may be taken all day.

Cascade Falls

This waterfall may be reached from Navajo Lake by driving eastward until the road forks south. From the fork, the waterfall is 1.7 miles away. Alternatively, turn off Highway 14 farther east and drive back to the waterfall. It is another jewel worth photographing, especially in the early summer.

Navajo Lake

Good photographs of the lake can be had at any time of day by driving along the south shore. To obtain attractive photographs from the highway, however, a morning drive is suggested. Autumn foliage at this high elevation puts on a spectacular show. The last 10 days of September are the peak time for capturing the explosion of shimmering gold, as the aspen leaves begin to change color.

Brian Head

The struggle for survival that plants make at this high altitude can be captured on film at any time of day. Since the view from here is mostly of distant objects, good scenic pictures can be made only on very clear days.

Zion Overview

Good photographs of the drainage of the North Fork of the Rio Virgin and the distant temples of Zion National Park can be had on a clear day from this spot.

An Alphabetical Listing of Southern Utah's Communities

ALTON

Elevation: 6,900 feet; population: 93.

Alton is a tiny community just a few miles southeast of the junction of Highways 89 and 14. Often unmarked on modernday maps, the village may be reached by turning off Highway 89, driving past several small lakes, and into a pretty valley. The imposing Paunsagunt Plateau serves as an attractive backdrop to the village, which nestles picturesquely in the valley.

As early as 1865, the lands near the headwaters of Kanab Creek were recognized by members of a scouting party as suitable for settlement. Consequently, between 1873 and 1874, approximately 10 families established ranches in a scattered community known as Upper Kanab. Their first post office was aptly named Ranch, Utah.

The need to provide a school for their children and a centralized meeting house prompted the families to consolidate and look for a suitable town site. The present location was surveyed in 1907, and construction of homes began shortly thereafter. The residents decided to give their community the descriptive name of Alton because of its unusually high elevation. Irrigated agriculture, livestock grazing, and lumbering still provide most of Alton's income. There are no visitor services here.

Just up the road at the junction of Highways 89 and 14 is what is variously known as the Gravel Springs junction, Gravel Pass, or the Long Valley junction. To the local residents it is simply the "Divide," a descriptive name, for the headwaters of the Sevier River and the Virgin River separate here. Waters flowing south of the pass enter the Parunuweap River, or the East Fork of the Virgin; those flowing north of it are carried via Tyler Creek into the Sevier. Since the gradient of the Virgin is many times greater than that of the Sevier, the "Divide" is slowly moving northward. Barring unforseen changes in topography, the turbulent Virgin will ultimately steal the headwaters of the quiet Sevier.

There is no positive record of the naming of the two rivers. The local Paiute Indians call the Virgin the *paruss*, meaning a "dirty or turbulent stream." They named the Sevier the *a-va-pa*, meaning "quiet waters" or "big placid river." Antonio Armijo, on January 1, 1830, called the Virgin River the Rio Severo, meaning "strict or severe," and suggesting a possible later exchange of the early Spanish names. Armijo's title seems akin to the Indian name for the Virgin, which in turn could be more understandably applied to the peaceful Sevier. On the other hand, there is a story that says the names of the two rivers were mixed up. For the moment, we can only speculate as to the origins of the two rivers' names.

The role of the turbulent Virgin River has been discussed elsewhere in this book, but the sedate, 225-mile-long Sevier is also important to Utah's history, for it provides water for irrigation in parts of six counties. Two of the Sevier's major tributaries, the Asay and Mammoth creeks, are born on the lofty Markagunt Plateau. These creeks are fed by numerous springs, some of them big enough to indicate underground channels in the soluble limestone that forms much of the plateau summit. At its terminus, the river formerly had a similar destiny. From the "Divide" it runs north for about 180 miles, makes a wide bend to the west, thence to the south, and thus reverses its direction of flow—one of the few rivers in the world to do this. Before white settlers arrived here, the waters ran into a dead lake and sank into the ground, known locally as "The Sevier Sinks"; however, the construction of the Yuba Dam has allowed farmers to tap these waters for irrigation of lands that would otherwise remain desert.

ASAY TOWN

Elevation 7,000 feet; population: 0.

The ghost town of Asay just off Highway 89 before Hatch was well named: the majority of the 10 or 12 families who settled along the banks of what became known, in 1872, as Asay Creek were descendants of Joseph Asay or relatives by

Fruita barn, Capitol Reef National Park

Strawberry Point

Elevation: 9,000 feet.

Strawberry Point, one of the southernmost projections of the Pink Cliffs on the Markagunt Plateau, is a superlative "extra" for visitors to southern Utah's Land of Color. Although the nine-mile road is rather narrow and requires the use of a low gear near its end, for the most part it is relatively straight and the surface graveled. A 500-foot trail leads from the parking area to a magnificent viewpoint that takes in the surrounding country.

To the north, the vivid reddish rock of the Wasatch Formation may be seen in several places, beautifully framed by deep green conifers and yellow-green quaking aspen. On the skyline rest three volcanic cones. The western horizon, which appears quite near, is interrupted by Pine Valley Mountain. To the left, the "temples" of Zion National Park are even closer, with majestic West Temple towering commandingly above all the others. Immediately below the point, and a bit farther to the left, an isolated natural bridge, the Temple Arch, is plainly visible.

The Grey Cliffs, which lie in the foreground on three sides, are richly vegetated with Transition Zone plants. Below them, to the south, lie the beveled tops of the White Cliffs. The pink-and-white sandstone ledges that mark the western edge of the plateau east of the Sevier Fault are easily recognizable. The few green fields noticeable from here are cultivated by residents of Long Valley. The dome of the Kaibab Upwarp, in which the Grand Canyon is carved, forms the far horizon. The terraces of the Paunsaugunt Plateau rise east to southeast in vertical succession. This Grand Staircase begins with the Vermilion Cliffs and ends with the watermelon-pink limestones of the Pink Cliffs to the north; the drab-colored volcanic debris of the Brian Head Formation caps the Pink Cliffs in many places.

marriage. Those people, and the rest of the original settlers, were exiles from the Muddy Mission in Nevada who had lived a year in the Long Valley towns.

Even though they developed farms and ranches along both forks of Asay Creek, the nucleus of their town was near the stream's confluence with the Sevier River, a few hundred yards west of the present concrete bridge over the creek. Here they constructed a schoolhouse, which served also as a church. Civil authorities established a post office in one of the homes.

They grazed cattle and horses on the nearby ranges and used the upper waters of the creek to run sawmills and shingle mills. Although wheat often did not mature in the short growing season at this high altitude, some grain was raised. As many as 20 families lived here at one time.

Asay Town seems to have died almost as abruptly as it was born. Continued cold weather discouraged the residents, and when one of their sawmills burned down in the late 1890s, they were further disheartened. In 1898, many people moved to the more favorable Big Horn country of Wyoming, when opportunities opened up there. A few families migrated elsewhere, and only a family or two remained within the county. By 1900 everyone had left the settlement. The log cabin built by James Little on his ranch west of the highway, about two miles south of Asay Creek, still stands. Aside from this structure and a small cemetery, little remains of Asay Town.

BOULDER

Elevation: 6,700 feet; population: 125.

The remote farming community of Boulder is located north of Escalante along Scenic Byway 12, a road that runs from Calf Creek up to Boulder, climbing through spectacular country en route to Capitol Reef National Park. The town may also be reached via the dirt Hell's Backbone Road from Escalante.

Boulder was first settled by ranchers in 1889 and became an important cattle and dairy center in the decades that followed. Access to this remote settlement was limited by the surrounding canyons and mountains. In 1942, Boulder was the last town in the United States still receiving mail by mule. Eventually, the construction of a rough road allowed motor vehicles to pass through and linked the town to the rest of Utah.

Anasazi Indian Village State Park is located in northeast Boulder. The site was set aside for protection after excavation revealed that a village uncovered here was once home to one of the largest Anasazi communities west of the Colorado River. The village is believed to have been occupied from A.D. 1050 to 1275, and then abandoned for unknown reasons. A fire destroyed much of the village before it was abandoned. Visitors follow a self-guided trail through the ruins and tour a museum which displays numerous Anasazi artifacts unearthed in the village. This is a pleasant spot for a picnic; no camping is allowed, though.

From Boulder, the paved Scenic Byway climbs through the thick forests of Boulder Mountain. Overlooks offer views of the canyons, the Waterpocket Fold at Capitol Reef, Calf Creek, Hell's backbone, and the Henry Mountains. Several U.S. Forest Service campgrounds may be found here. Highway 12 joins Highway 24 close to Torrey; from here it is an 11-mile drive east to Capitol Reef National Park. If well prepared and the weather is good, travelers may also choose to take the unpaved Burr Trail Road from Boulder to Capitol Reef's southern district via the Waterpocket Fold and Circle Cliffs.

BRIAN HEAD

Elevation: 9,850 feet; population: 109.

The high-country resort of Brian Head, located 14 miles from Parowan on a year-round section of Highway 143, is the highest town in Utah. It has some of the best skiing in the state and plenty of attractive hotels, condominiums, restaurants, and other visitor facilities. Snow is abundant here until well into late spring.

The portion of Highway 143 that links up with Highway 14 just past Cedar Breaks National Monument generally opens up in mid-May, depending on the weather. This Scenic Byway, taking in the red rock of the lava-topped Markagunt Plateau, is popular with summer visitors, who enjoy driving through the breathtaking high country. Brian Head can also be reached year-round from Highway 89 to the southeast, via Panguitch.

The summit of Brian Head, which towers above the town, is 11,307 feet high. It is composed principally of ash, tuff, breccia, and the other volcanic materials that make up the Brian Head Formation—here capped with a resistant layer of light-colored lava, known as rhyolite. A climb down the west face reveals a variety of once molten rock.

A visit to the high platform of Brian Head, which is accessible via an unpaved road, provides beautiful, sweeping vistas of the area. In the foreground, to the north, lie the Paiute Highlands, shattered by at least nine faults. Beyond these tablelands is the desert of the Great Basin, watered at its eastern edge by the streams from the high plateaus. To the north, and a bit to the east, one can see the magnificent peaks of the Beaver Mountains, part of the Tushar Range; they are the remains of a past epoch of profound volcanism. The view to the east and south overlooks the east-tilted platform of the Markagunt Plateau, capped here and there with relatively recent volcanic cones and fissure flows of Quaternary Epoch lava. Beyond the Markagunt, and bordered by the Pink Cliffs, the western edges of

the Paunsagunt and Sevier plateaus are in view. Still farther east, the elevated platforms of the Aquarius and Table Cliffs plateaus rise above the level of their western neighbors. In the immediate foreground, directly to the south, is the highly eroded, pale pink facade of Cedar Breaks National Monument.

BRYCE CANYON NATIONAL PARK

Elevation: 6,600 to 9,100 feet; population: 50.

Bryce Canyon is not really a canyon; rather, it is an amphitheater cut into the eastern edge of the Paunsagunt Plateau. Here, a whole host of eerie, reddish rock formations have been carved out of the rock by the action of rain drops and other erosional forces.

The Paiutes called this place *unka-timpe-wa-wince, pock-ich,* which means "red rocks standing like men in a bowl-shaped canyon," an apt description for the strangely eroded forms crowding along the edge of these cliffs. Although the early Mormon explorers probably saw this scenic jewel, they made no note of it, possibly because dramatic landscapes are commonplace here, and these settlers had a good deal other than scenery on their minds. Even the diary of James Andrus, who led an army of 60 men through this region in 1866, makes no mention of it. Members of both the Wheeler and Powell surveys visiting the area in the 1870s were more enthusiastic in their response and penned glowing descriptions of the unusual scenery. To this day, the magnificent account of Bryce written by Captain C. E. Dutton of the Powell expedition remains unexcelled.

The parent rock here is largely the freshwater limestone of the Claron member of the

Wasatch Formation, which owes its beautiful coloration to small amounts of iron and manganese oxides in the rock. Although alternate freezing and thawing, the intrusive roots of growing plants, and the cutting action of intermittent streams have been important agents in sculpting the rock, the principal erosive agent at Bryce is rainfall. The bizarre multitude of grotesquely shaped rocks, often called "hoodoos," that descend from these cliffs owe their shapes mostly to the way erosion has worn away rocks of different composition and hardness.

The edge of the plateau into which this unusual amphitheater has been carved is located along the Paunsagunt Fault. Here, the earth's crust has cracked along a geological fault and the land to the east uplifted along the break to create another plateau, fully 2,000 feet above Bryce. The

Queen's Garden, Bryce Canyon National Park

Bryce Canyon Photography Tips

An observant professional once wisely remarked, "Bryce Canyon is a color photographer's paradise." As this is most assuredly true, and also because lighting conditions fluctuate so greatly with the seasons and with time of day, it is obviously impossible to give complete information. Professional and advanced amateur photographers have taken some wonderful photographs of individual sculpted figures from along the trails within the amphitheater. Some views make good backlit shots, with Queen Victoria, Tower Bridge, Oastler's Castle, Fairy Castle, and a host of others providing excellent subject material. Bryce offers the opportunity to exercise individual artistry and to try out different shots.

In spite of the complexities, there are areas where everyone, even the beginner, can take deeply satisfying photographs. Remember that the light is "hot" here and that exposures that may seem as much as a full stop under may be "right on" during much of the day.

MORNING PHOTOGRAPHS

Fairyland—A bit to the right of the trail head, there is a pine tree with forked roots which makes excellent frame material. Early morning possibilities here are excellent.

Sunrise Point—To get the best general morning shots, hike along the trail towards the Queen's Garden some 300 yards to where it levels off, and then shoot toward the Queen's Garden.

Sunset Point—Shoot either toward the north or the south. A stroll down the steps on the Navajo Trail and a short, level hike through the tunnels in either direction increases photographic possibilities.

Inspiration Point—Some photographers insist that this is the most desirable point from which to shoot the Silent City. It is good from early morning until 11 A.M.

Bryce Point—Shoot here during the morning hours.

Agua Canyon—Early morning is best.

MIDDAY PHOTOGRAPHS

From 10:00 A.M. until 3:00 P.M., good east-facing general views in such areas as the Queen's Garden and Fairyland Canyon. All the trails afford many possibilities, but the Fairyland Canyon, Campbell Canyon, Queen's Garden, and Peek-a-boo trails are outstanding.

AFTERNOON PHOTOGRAPHS

Two afternoons are really necessary to do it all. If only one is possible, greater satisfaction will probably be obtained by staying in the area of the main canyon.

Fairyland—Best around 4:00 P.M. Shoot down the canyon.

Sunrise Point—Good from middle to late afternoon from points near the head of the Queen's Garden Trail.

Sunset Point—Good shots may be obtained here in both directions all afternoon. When shooting toward the Silent City, however, shade your lens from the sun.

Inspiration Point—While good photographs may be obtained here all afternoon, the most dramatic light occurs during the later hours.

Bryce Point—The Paria Valley, and the Table Cliffs beyond, may be photographed all day long, but the best afternoon picture of Bryce Canyon is obtained shortly before sunset.

Natural Bridge—The average lens will not get it all in, regardless of how hard you try. A wide angle lens, however, will do the trick. This shot is only good in the early afternoon, until 4:00 P.M. in midsummer.

Agua Canyon—Good results from shooting down this colorful canyon any time in the afternoon.

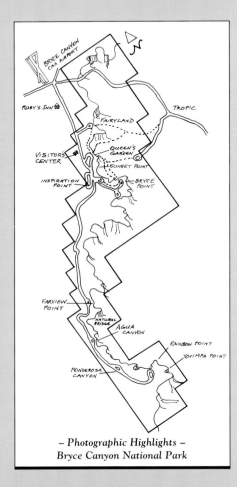

– Photographic Highlights –
Bryce Canyon National Park

Rainbow Point—Good from mid-afternoon until the late hours.

Yovimpa Point—The best photographs are taken here in the late hours. Shoot toward the west and southwest.

pink ledges across the valley to the east are the Table Cliffs. The forested summit of the Aquarius Plateau lies to the north of these cliffs.

Between Bryce Canyon and the Table Cliffs lies the Paria Valley, a product of the action of the Paria River and its tributaries. The Paria is, itself, a tributary of the Colorado River. Thus, through these streams, the silt-laden raindrops from Bryce Canyon may be borne through Lake Powell and Glen Canyon Dam, all the way to where the Colorado River empties into the sea.

The fantastically carved plateau, while used seasonally by Indians, was first viewed by white men around 1876, when a Scottish Mormon convert named Ebenezer Bryce built a cabin at the mouth of the canyon and raised livestock here. Bryce had been in southern Utah for a number of years and had supervised construction of the unusual church in Pine Valley. Like his contemporaries, he was little concerned with the scenery, and indeed commented that the endless clusters of hoodoos, spires, and other eroded rocks made the canyon "a hell of a place to lose a cow." Locals soon began calling the area Bryce's Canyon.

For years, Bryce Canyon remained an undiscovered wonderland. In 1905, it was designated part of a national forest set aside for protection under President Theodore Roosevelt's national forest program. As a consequence, a few more people became aware of the delicate, pastel-colored, stone sculptures found here. Not until 1915, however—when Will Humphrey, the new forest supervisor, saw its potential and secured funds for a primitive road—did Bryce Canyon receive much publicity. Soon thereafter it was visited by several writers whose vivid narratives were published in state newspapers and national magazines.

In 1916 Ruben C. Syrett built a ranch house near the present site of Ruby's Inn, just outside the park entrance. Soon thereafter, having been told of Bryce Canyon by a neighboring rancher, Syrett and his young family made a Sunday visit to the rim. They were so impressed by what they saw that they began to publicize the canyon's beauties at every opportunity and also hosted many of its visitors. By 1919, the Syretts had obtained permission from the state to build a lodge, the Tourist Rest, near the rim. That year also, the Utah legislature lobbied Congress to create the Temple of the Gods National Monument, a title that the local forest men felt more appropriate than the name Bryce Canyon.

The matter was referred to the National Park Service, who were at first unwilling to grant the state's request. They proposed, instead, that Utah set the area aside as part of what would be Utah State Park. When the state declined, the president intervened and proclaimed the area Bryce Canyon National Monument in 1923. That same year, the newly formed Utah Parks Company acquired Ruby Syrett's holdings and began construction of what would become Bryce Lodge. Syrett moved back to his ranch and built Ruby's Inn, which is still in operation and has now been expanded into a large, modern hotel, providing such attractions as rodeos, helicopter rides, and slide shows. The post office subsequently established there serves the area year-round.

In 1924, Congress authorized Utah National Park, an enlarged area that included Bryce Canyon National Monument. Not until 1928, however, was Bryce Canyon National Park established and given its present name. Three years later Congress enlarged it to its present size of 35,835 acres.

The historic Bryce Lodge, now run by TW Services, remains immensely popular with visitors to the park. Two campgrounds are operated by the park service. Thirty-five miles of paved, all-weather roads with overlooks make sightseeing pleasant and comfortable. An excellent way to explore the park is either to take a horseback ride or hike along any one of the splendid trails that lead from various points along the rim into the depths of the canyon. The park is open year-round.

CANNONVILLE

Elevation: 6,000 feet; population 131.

From various points along the rim of Bryce Canyon you can see parts of several small towns in the Paria Valley, locally referred to as "under the dump." The histories of all towns in this region are intimately connected. Minor points of disagreement exist between the different available accounts, probably because some of the early records were destroyed by fire.

It is known for certain that a party of Mormon scouts who entered the valley in 1866 recognized that it was suitable for settlement. Later, perhaps as early as 1868, riders investigated the region searching for grazing lands. Finding abundant forage, they began grazing the Kanarra Coop cattle herd from a base in the little town of Kanarraville. By 1874 two of the herdsmen and their families had settled at the junction of Paria Creek and Henrieville Creek, in a place they called Clifton (Cliff Town), known locally as "Wooden Shoe." Shortly thereafter, other settlers joined the group.

Because of the limited amount of arable land at Clifton, residents broke ground for their farms a few miles up both forks of the stream. Diversion of water onto these lands and a couple of dry years caused the creeks to dry up before the water reached their homes, requiring residents to haul water for household use. As a consequence, some folks decided to move up the streams to a

Chimney Rock, Capitol Reef National Park

more favorable location nearer their farm lands. Cannonville was one of the villages that resulted.

In 1876, some families moved up the Paria about three miles and selected a town site, which they named Cannonville, after George Q. Cannon, a contemporary Mormon Church leader. According to all acounts, browse and forage were so plentiful that the livestock industry flourished.

The little town grew rapidly and for a time was very prosperous. A short time later, however, overgrazing of the semiarid land had destroyed much of the protective covering of vegetation that held the desert soil. Subsequent flooding carried away much of the already limited agricultural land. Because the depleted range would not sustain the large numbers of sheep and cattle that had been introduced, this industry steadily dwindled. Today agriculture, lumbering, and some employment at Bryce Canyon provide the principal sources of income. The little town is now the gateway to Kodachrome Basin State Park. While it is possible to see some of the Paria Valley towns from the rim of Bryce Canyon, it is difficult, if not impossible, to see Cannonville from there.

CAPITOL REEF NATIONAL PARK

Elevation: 6,000 to 9,000 feet; population: approx. 40

Capitol Reef National Park lies in the northeastern corner of southern Utah's Land of Color, amid magnificent high desert country that also includes the Escalante canyonlands, Boulder Mountain, and the Paria Wilderness to the south. The 378-square-mile park was set aside because it encompasses much of the 100-mile-long Waterpocket Fold, a spectacular, eroded upwarp in the earth's surface that runs through south-central Utah.

The Capitol Reef (named by explorers who thought it looked like an ocean reef capped by domes reminiscent of the U.S. Capitol) is a particularly scenic, 10-mile section of the Fold just south of the Fremont River. Geologists believe that it was formed during the Laramide Orogeny about 65 million years ago, when the Pacific plate ground against the adjoining North American plate, sending shock waves eastward. The crustal movements buckled the thick sedimentary rocks that had been deposited by millenia of seas, rivers, tidal flats, and sand dunes, creating a series of monoclines, or upwarps. The Waterpocket Fold (named for the water that collects in depressions in the sandstone) is considered a particularly spectacular example.

A 20-mile, paved scenic drive, which crosses the crest of Capitol Reef, starts at the visitor center in Fruita and follows Highway 24, winding beneath towering Navajo and Wingate Sandstone and paralleling the heavily vegetated banks of the Fremont River. An unpaved scenic drive extends south from the visitor center, allowing visitors excellent views of the Waterpocket Fold. The Notom-Bullfrog Road on the east side of the Fold runs southward as far as Bull-frog Marina in Glen Canyon National Recreation Area; about halfway down, it joins the famous old Burr Trail Road, which allows travelers to drive westward to Boulder. The remote, highly eroded northern exposure of the monocline may be reached by an unpaved road, which is only viable by four-wheel-drive vehicle or on foot. Here 500-foot spires of Entrada Sandstone silently bear witness to the turbulent geological forces that buffeted this landscape. Later volcanic eruptions, which built Thousand Lake Mountain to the north, were responsible too for intrusions into the sedimentary rock, causing it to bulge into laccolithic mountains like the Henrys in the distance. Lava was carried by glaciation into the area.

As the Colorado Plateau rose it was subjected to erosion, which formed the natural bridges, arches, spires, cliffs, and hogbacks found in the park. Particularly striking are the 1,500-foot, colorful, rolling strata on the southern exposure of the Fold, which reaches to Bullfrog Basin at Lake Powell. Domes, natural arches, and natural bridges formed by wind and water also characterize this section.

The tall cliffs of Capitol Reef sheltered the pithouse dwellings of the Fremont Indians, who hunted, gathered, and grew hardy maize crops along the river here between A.D. 700 and 1275. Like their Anasazi neighbors, the Fremont developed a significant culture, perhaps best known for its striking rock art, clay figurines, and specially adapted clothing, such as moccasins with heels made from the dewclaw of a deer. In the 13th century, the Fremont mysteriously disappeared, perhaps forced away by severe drought, diminishing resources, and encroachment by Shoshonean cultures. The exiles may have joined the Paiutes who had started to use the area, or perhaps the Rio Grande pueblos to the south absorbed them. No one knows for sure.

After centuries of use by Paiutes and Utes who hunted and gathered here, Anglo cattle ranchers and prospectors "discovered" the fertile river at the heart of this great barrier in the late 19th century. In the 1880s, 10 Mormon families established the settlement of Junction (later Fruita) by the river and supplied travelers and settlers in remote communities with fruit grown along the floodplain. The residents also built a little schoolhouse, which may still be seen today.

Parts of Capitol Reef were protected as a national monument in 1937. But some residents remained until the National Park Service bought them out as part of an expansion in 1968. The monument was further expanded and made a national park in 1971. No food, lodging, or supplies are available in the park, but accommodations and stores may be found in Fishlake and Dixie national forests and communities nearby. The park service maintains a campground in the orchards at Fruita; visitors may pick fruit for personal consumption in season for a reasonable price per pound.

CEDAR BREAKS NATIONAL MONUMENT

Elevation: 10,350 feet (Point Supreme); population: 0.

The Paiutes called this multicolored amphitheater *un-cap-i-cun-ump*, meaning "circle of painted cliffs" or "circle of red cliffs." It was given its present name by Mormon settlers who mistakenly called the abundant juniper trees "cedars" and referred to the clearing in this forested high country as "the breaks."

Cedar Breaks has a geological story similar to that of Bryce Canyon; both are amphitheaters cut in the edge of an uplifted plateau, and both have been carved by the action of raindrops,

which have slowly but relentlessly eaten their way into the soluble limestone, forming fantastically shaped rocks. The Pink Cliffs made up of the Claron member of the Wasatch Formation are thicker here, measuring over 1,300 feet high, and somewhat more colorful. In addition, more than 700 feet of the Grey Cliffs, composed of the Kaiparowits Formation, may be seen in the bottom of the canyon, bringing the total visible depth of these dramatic ledges to more than 2,000 feet.

Cedar Breaks became a national monument by presidential proclamation on August 27, 1933. At Point Supreme, a visitor center with a superb "picture window" view of the cliffs features exhibits about the monument's geology and biology. Park naturalists give interpretive talks during summer and fall. Highway 14, a Scenic Byway beginning at Cedar City and ending at Highway 89, passes the monument just to the south. State Road 148, running through the monument, connects Highway 14 with State Road 143 to the north. Turnoffs along State Road 143 lead to splendid viewpoints at Sunset View, Chessman Ridge Overlook, and North View. Visitors cross the Brian Head lava flow east of the monument. State Road 143 is closed by snow from as early as late September to as late as early June, during which time the hushed monument becomes a playground for snowmobilers and skiers. A campground, run by the National Park Service, is also open seasonally.

Cedar Breaks is celebrated for its glorious displays of wildflowers, which bloom in the summer at this high elevation. Two easy hiking trails offer wonderful views of the plateau's strangely weathered facade. A special treat at Spectra Point is a stand of bristlecone pines, gnarled old trees able to withstand the extreme temperatures of this high altitude. They are

considered the earth's oldest living trees and grow in just a few special locations in the American West. Experienced hikers may wish to tackle the Rattlesnake Creek Trail, a U.S. Forest Service backcountry trail down into the canyon. Before attempting the steep trail, talk to a ranger at the Cedar Breaks Visitor Center.

One and a half miles west of the Cedar Breaks junction on Highway 14, the Zion Overview, a wide lookout area set amid some very young topography, provides the best view of the birthplace of the North Fork of the Rio Virgin. In the middle foreground lies the Kolob Terrace, a beveled platform of Grey Cliffs of the Wahweap and Straight Cliffs formations, into which the tributaries have incised deep channels. Beyond the Kolob is a second platform, the tops of the

Point Supreme, Cedar Breaks National Monument

Cedar Breaks Photography Tips

Despite its small size, Cedar Breaks National Monument is a photographer's dream, particularly during July and early August. At that time, Nature sets off the delicately hued, ornate rock sculptures at cliff's edge and the photogenic cloud-scapes above them with carpets of rainbow-colored subalpine wildflowers in the meadows—a sight not to be missed.

During most of the day at this high altitude, the sun-light is so intense that photographs of the light-colored canyon can easily be over-exposed. Photographers are advised to under-expose their film slightly between 9:30 A.M. and 4:00 P.M. to get the best results.

The lush floral displays make very satisfying photo-graphs. Many of the delicate, translucent flowers can be backlit to good effect. In full sunlight, exposures a full stop more than those used for photographs of the scenery have given highly successful closeups. Since this floral display is seasonal, ask park rangers at the visitor center at Point Supreme for advice about what is in bloom. The following are some suggestions for good scenic views.

MORNING PHOTOGRAPHS

Point Supreme—Spectra Point to the west is in full sunlight. Late morning, photographs in the direction of Brian Head to the north are possible. Tower Arch may be photographed with a telephoto lens. Ask a park naturalist how to locate the arch.

Sunset View—Good pictures may be taken here almost any time except during the late afternoon.

Chessmen Ridge Overlook—Early morning pictures shot from here are good, although the contrast may be great. Good frames are available all day long on either side of this viewpoint.

North View—The north side of Chessmen Ridge, with its deep green conifers set in sharp contrast to the pastel colors of the limestone, provides good photographic material all day.

AFTERNOON PHOTOGRAPHS

Spectra Point (Point Perfection)—Reached over a foot trail beginning in the visitor center parking lot; this point is an excellent spot from which to take panoramic shots of

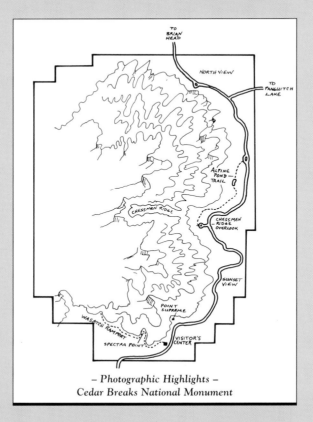

– Photographic Highlights –
Cedar Breaks National Monument

the canyon and the ancient bristlecone pine growing here. The trail continues beyond Spectra Point along the Wasatch Rampart to the monument boundary. Although the return trip can be tiring at this high altitude, superlative viewpoints and photographic gems along the trail make the trip worthwhile.

Point Supreme—Photographs here are good all after-noon but are best about 3:00 P.M. or later.

Sunset View—As the name suggests, the best pictures are to be had near 3:00 P.M. or later.

Chessmen Ridge Overlook—Photographs taken of the view to the north or south are good all afternoon. Step back for frames.

North View—This vista works well all afternoon, although some shots are best in the early evening.

Navajo and Carmel formations that make up the White Cliffs. Here, the streams have joined forces in carving Zion Canyon. Many of Zion's famous monoliths are plainly visible. On all but the haziest days, one can see the tops of the Vermil-ion Cliffs beyond the White Cliffs. On a very clear day, the great dome of the Kaibab Plateau in the far distance is discernible. Turn to the south-ern Utah geology chart on page 23 for further information.

CEDAR CITY

Elevation: 5,800 feet; population: 15,443.

Before the white man came, the present site of Cedar City was used by Paiute Indians, who called it *we-see-ap-to*, meaning "a grove of scrub cedars." Then, in 1849, Parley P. Pratt's party of explorers found rich deposits of iron ore nine miles north-west of the present town, and Pratt selected what was to become the city's first town site.

In 1851, shortly after the settling of Parowan, one of the early settlers, Peter Shirts, found coal while exploring the Little Muddy Creek (now Coal Creek, paralleling much of the road to Cedar Breaks National Monument). Encouraged by this find, a group from Parowan moved to the site in early November, made preliminary surveys, and named their village site Cedar City after a large clump of juniper trees they found there, (incor-rectly referred to as "cedars"). Within a month a company of English, Scottish, and Welsh miners and iron workers arrived in Parowan. Once they had organized, they proceeded to Cedar City and immediately began to "fort up" on the north side of Coal Creek. By February 1852, Cedar City had incorporated and a municipal government had been established.

The company devoted its energies toward

"forting, fencing, ditching, farming, gardening, and prospecting, not forgetting the prime object of making iron." Their efforts in the latter objective were rewarded on September 30 when they tapped the first blast furnace and cast the first iron. The arrival of new settlers in October led the residents to survey new land and provide lots for the new arrivals on the south side of the creek (this eventually became the present town site).

Meanwhile, missionaries had journeyed to England to select converts to run the new iron industry and to procure money to finance it. In April 1852, these men organized the Deseret Iron Company in Liverpool and helped the converts obtain passage to America. Arriving in Cedar City in November, the immigrants purchased the holdings of the earlier workers and by March of the following year, using charcoal as fuel, had produced 2,500 pounds of excellent iron.

When the Walker Indian War broke out in July 1853, the townspeople prepared to defend themselves against Indian attacks. Then, in September, disastrous floods down Coal Creek seriously damaged the iron works and other installations. As a result, Cedar City residents spent much of the rest of the year, and all of the one that followed, rebuilding the iron works, opening a coal mine, and constructing coke ovens.

The new works ran well for a couple of weeks, and then blew out; continued problems led eventually to a permanent cessation of operations. Fortunately, however, the settlers had not relied entirely on the iron industry, but had organized cooperative herds, grist mills, tanneries, and furniture establishments. They had also built a wool carding machine and a woolen factory. Farming and dairying in the valley soon became profitable on an ongoing basis, helped by the introduction of alfalfa for livestock feed in the 1870s.

In May 1897, at the request of the city, the Utah state legislature authorized the construction of a teacher training school in Cedar City. The resulting Branch Normal College, first established as a branch of the State University, later became a branch of the Utah State Agricultural College. Today, the college is a four-year educational institution known as Southern Utah University.

In 1923, the Union Pacific Railroad ran a branch line into Cedar City through the Iron Springs district. In the same year, the Columbia Steel Company began to mine and ship the rich deposits of iron ore. Twenty years later, both industries received another stimulus with the construction of the Geneva Steel Plant in Provo, Utah. The growing steel industry in California was also making increasingly large demands on the ore supply here. In order to meet those needs, companies adopted the strip mining method of extraction, necessitating the removal of heavy overburdens of gangue (metallic veins or passages) from the ore beds. Although there is still abundant iron ore in the Cedar City vicinity, mining has almost disappeared in recent years due to the pressure of global market forces. For a while, rich deposits of limestone and gypsum provided raw materials for a plaster mill, and quaking aspen cut high on the Markagunt Plateau fed the Excelsior Mill. A rocket fuel plant was built in recent years west of town, but the livestock industry continues to play an important part in the economy, with both the nearby valleys and mountains providing good forage in season.

Today, Cedar City is best known as the home of the world-famous Utah Shakespearean Festival, hosted by SUU since 1964. The popular, nine-week festival is held annually in July, August, and September and features both obscure and well-known Shakespearean plays performed on a replica of the original Globe Theatre stage in England, as well as other Elizabethan entertainments. The Utah Summer Games, patterned after the Olympic Games and held in late June, is also a big draw, with athletes from all over Utah and even from Russia competing.

Cedar City is also home to the Iron Mission State Park, a museum that tells the story of Iron County from the earliest Paiute Indian residents to the establishment of the Iron Mission here. The museum contains many pioneer artifacts, a display of horse-drawn vehicles, and the excellent William R. Palmer collection of Paiute baskets and artifacts. The administrative offices of Utah's Southern Paiute Tribe are located just across from the state park, and the town is home to a sizeable Southern Paiute population.

Cedar City is a popular base for visitors journeying between Zion, Bryce, and Arizona's

Coal Creek Canyon

A drive along Highway 14 between Cedar City and Cedar Breaks through Coal Creek Canyon brings visitors into contact with rocks belonging to each of the three geologic eras (Paleozoic to Cenozoic) found in the canyons, plateaus, and valleys of southern Utah's color country. Here, one may see all the rock formations shown on the geology chart on page 23 within the space of 21.5 miles.

The sedimentary strata exposed along the road were originally deposited from a succession of streams, oceans, wind-blown dunes, and lakes, and coal was formed in ancient bogs and marshes. The road passes over bends, folds, and eight faults. The interpretation of such complex geology is beyond the scope of this book. Those interested in finding out more about southern Utah geology should refer to *A Roadside Geology of Utah* by Halka Chronic, published by Mountain Press, and available at bookstores in Zion and Bryce national parks and at Cedar Breaks National Monument.

Grand Canyon national parks, Cedar Breaks and Pipe Spring national monuments, as well as for those exploring Color Country's many other state parks, recreation areas, and scenic drives.

CENTRAL

Elevation: 5,200 feet; population: 175.

The several lava flows located in Washington County have been mixed blessings for its settlers. The downward rush of many of the youthful streams that drain the area have been temporarily delayed by some of the lava flows: Pine Valley, Veyo, Hurricane, and La Verkin all rest on soils that have been deposited atop or behind these igneous barriers. But the same properties that make the lava so resistant to stream erosion also cause serious problems. Canyons cut through lava are straight-walled, and lava strenuously resists the efforts of man to alter its natural state.

The first men to recognize the agricultural potential at Central, a pleasant alpine settlement close to Pine Valley, faced some of these obstacles. The irrigation ditch they dug to the "gulch" where they hoped to take water from Santa Clara Creek was excavated with relative ease. But the lava canyon where the stream was entrenched was another matter. Since there was insufficient timber to make a flume to carry the water out of the chasm, the entire project had to be abandoned.

Then, in 1904, Henry Holt studied the abandoned ditch and determined that by tunneling to a certain point and blasting a quarter-mile-long ditch through the resistant black rock, water could be brought out onto the land. Eventually, he interested enough of his neighbors to raise the necessary capital to get the work accomplished. As a result, by February 1909 the proper applications had been made for the water rights, the land had been surveyed, and applications for homesteads filed. A post office was built and given the name Central because of the village's location approximately midway between Veyo and Pine Valley. A public building, which served as school, church, and recreation center, was erected later. Central is still an agricultural community, whose income from the limited acreage of irrigated land is supplemented by that from dry farms, dependant upon rainfall to sustain their yield.

COLORADO CITY
(SHORT CREEK)

Elevation: 5,000 feet; population: 2,426.

In 1961, when residents of southern Utah saw road signs with arrows pointing toward Short Creek bearing a new name, Colorado City, they were not particularly surprised. This private little town astride the Utah-Arizona boundary had drawn the unwelcome attention of the outside world from the 1930s on. Now, a new name (*colorado* means "reddish" or "ruddy" in Spanish—a reference to the Vermilion Cliffs) opened the dusty little community to public scrutiny once more, bringing back a flood of memories for many area residents.

This part of the rugged Arizona Strip region north of the Grand Canyon was first settled in October 1861, when William B. Maxwell, a Mormon settler "called" to Grafton as part of the Dixie Mission, found perennial springs in the tributary canyons to Short Creek. Maxwell built a ranch at the mouth of Maxwell Canyon and raised cattle on what was then good grassland. In the late 19th century, many weary travelers on the Arizona Strip stopped by on their way through the area.

Except for notations made in the diaries of travelers, Short Creek received little attention until 1908 when two enterprising men from Richfield, Utah, Jacob M. Lauritzen and William Rust, conceived the idea of bringing water from the Virgin River through the sandstone ledges several miles northwest of Canaan Ranch, in order to irrigate the level benchland. The many springs that fed Short Creek, they proposed, would supply good drinking water for the new town.

The necessary land titles were secured, and by 1910 Rust had moved his family into a rock-lined dugout until a suitable home could be erected. Lauritzen's family found temporary shelter in three tents. The project fell through due to lack of capital; irrigation agriculture, therefore, was limited to the lands made arable by Short Creek's scanty flow.

Undeterred, by 1912 several families had joined the settlement, necessitating the construction of a small school. In June 1914 they were granted a post office, and a few more families moved in. Still others came in 1918, a year after the elder Lauritzen had turned his property over to his sons and taken other employment. Rust had sold out earlier. After a few years of ranching, during which time they planted fruit trees, set out vineyards, and raised vegetable gardens, the younger Lauritzens followed their father to California, where he had moved to improve his situation.

Among the newcomers who followed Lauritzen and Rust into Short Creek were some who came from parents who, despite the manifesto officially adopted by the Mormon Church, had continued to live in plural marriages. About 1924, a settler from such a family took a second wife and succeeded in converting other residents to the practice. Polygamy thus gained a foothold in Short Creek.

Early in the 1930s, two independent influences swelled the population from 61 persons to 180. The first of these was the onset of the Depression, which prompted the temporary return of the Lauritzens. They renovated their abandoned homes and used the still scanty, but now priceless, water to cultivate new gardens and to revive their neglected vineyards and orchards.

Meanwhile, the resurgence in polygamy had reached such proportions in Short Creek and elsewhere as to cause alarm and to provoke action by the Mormon Church in both Arizona and Utah. In 1933 and 1934, the Church excommunicated members of the sect. That autumn, the threat of legal action in northern Utah prompted a number of leaders of the movement to visit Short Creek and make plans to move there. On March 14, 1935, the Utah legislature amended existing legislation making cohabitation a felony instead of a misdemeanor. The act took effect two months later. Shortly thereafter, leaders and many members of the organization moved to Short Creek. But before year's end, Arizona officials had arrested three suspects, convicted two, and sent them to jail.

Short Creek lost some of its citizens following the hard winter of 1936–1937. The cold and the isolation resulting from deep snow not only made necessary such emergency measures as chopping green juniper trees for fuel but also led to serious food shortages. By 1941, however, the hamlet was attracting newcomers again. During the following year the leaders of the sect brought most of their members into a communal organization, which they call the United Effort.

Despite a raid by the FBI in 1944, and con-

victions in Utah that were sustained by the Utah Supreme Court, members of the United Effort continued to move to Short Creek. With the consequent increase in school population and higher taxes, officials in Mohave County were faced squarely with one consequence of plural marriage. In 1951, the Arizona legislature appropriated funds to investigate the practice, and in 1953 to deal with it. On July 25, 1953, nearly 100 state troopers, deputies, welfare workers, members of the press, and others moved out in two directions from Kingman, Arizona, converging on Short Creek in the predawn hours of Sunday, July 26. Overnight, the Short Creek story became a national news item.

Although the raid had been carefully planned and executed, its surprise element boomeranged. When the arresting officers arrived, they found the suspects assembled in front of their tiny school singing *America the Beautiful*. The women and children were taken to Phoenix, Arizona, and the men brought to trial in Kingman. Rumor has it that the governor of Arizona was swamped with letters expressing sympathy for the Short Creek people. Ultimately, the men posted bond and were released on probation. In 1956, Utah officials arrested one woman and for a time separated her from her children.

By the early 1960s, 100 years after Maxwell first established his ranch, there were signs that Short Creek, now renamed Colorado City, would escape from its semi-isolation with the completion of Highway 59. The population of the hamlet was still swelling. A privately endowed high school had been added, housed in adobe buildings constructed by the students from local lumber sawn in their own mill. Modern, spacious trailer houses were occupied by some new residents. Others were building new homes and improving older ones.

Coral Pink Sand Dunes State Park

Today, the town is continuing to grow, with new homes under construction all the time.

To many people, the most amazing aspect of this growth is that it has occurred without any visible increase in the town's inherently feeble economic base. A transmission line now brings electrical power to the community, allowing irrigation water to be pumped onto cultivated fields; lumber from the Kaibab Plateau to the south feeds the timber industry; and the industrial park at Hildale, Utah, just west of the town, has also brought greater economic development in recent years. But despite its proximity to Highway 59, which links Fredonia, Arizona, and Hurricane, Utah, Colorado City remains relatively untouched by the outside world.

CORAL PINK SAND DUNES STATE PARK

Elevation: 6,000 feet.

In a valley 14 miles northwest of Kanab and 11 miles from Highway 89, coral-colored grains of sand carried by the wind have piled up into large dunes that reach several hundred feet high in places. The area has been set aside as the 3,700-acre Coral Pink Sand Dunes State Park and is an excellent area for riding off-road vehicles, hiking, photography, and frolicking in the dunes.

When the United States Congress authorized the construction of the Glen Canyon Dam early in 1956, residents of the Paria Valley hoped for the construction of a short-cut to the damsite from northern Utah via a valley in the East Kaibab Monocline carved by Cottonwood Creek. The decision of the Utah State Road Commission to build an alternate route around the Vermilion Cliffs (now Highway 89), while disappointing, only served to arouse the residents' pioneer spirit. Spearheaded by Samuel Pollack, the people of Paria Valley gathered materials, secured over $5,000 in donations, rented and borrowed equipment, and went to work building their own road. This road survives today, beginning as a paved road in Cannonville and leading southward, past Kodachrome Basin, where it continues as an unpaved road until reaching Highway 89.

Without thought of compensation, many residents gave freely of their energy and skills to build the road. Mr. Pollack, lacking the services of an engineer, drew on his long knowledge of the terrain and laid out the road himself, donating 100 days of his time. The road was begun in June 1957 and dedicated in September of that year. With such limited resources it was inevitable that the route chosen was not always ideal. In some places it is too narrow, in others the turns are too sharp, and in several it is alarmingly steep. In wet weather, it is advisable to enquire locally about the condition of the road. Under all conditions it must be traveled at a reasonable speed and with due caution.

Conspicuous east of Highway 89, between the road to the old Paria town site and the Kaibab Gulch, is a 150-mile-long fold in the rock known locally as the Coxcomb (or more properly the East Kaibab Monocline), which rises as much as 1,150 feet above the Paria River on its eastern flank. The Jurassic strata, which are so vividly displayed here, are tilted at angles of up to 60 degrees. Farther south, in Arizona, the monocline blends into and becomes part of the Kaibab Upwarp.

In Houserock Valley, north of the Kaibab Gulch, the western valley wall is composed of Kaibab limestone, which is overlaid in places by patches of Moenkopi shale. The balance of the Triassic rocks is buried beneath alluvium in the valley floor. The alluvium conceals a remarkable thinning of Triassic sediments in the vicinity of Kaibab Gulch, suggesting faulting and perhaps overthrusting.

To the east the Coxcomb is cut through by Kaibab Creek, which is now paralleled by Highway 89. In the walls of Kaibab Creek Canyon from west to east stands the Navajo Sandstone, covered in sequence by the Carmel, Entrada, Winsor, and Dakota formations. Some, or all, of these deposits are conspicuous alongside the highway between the Paria River and the Glen Canyon Dam. To the north, in the vicinity of Glen Canyon City, the blue-grey marine shales of the Tropic Formation are overlaid by the Straight Cliffs.

With the notable exception of Cottonwood Creek, a later stream that has cut its valley in less resistant sediments of the East Kaibab Monocline, neither the Paria River nor most of its other tributaries have been influenced by the monocline. It is likely that the monocline was upwarped prior to the deposition of the Tertiary rocks represented by the pink Wasatch limestone at Bryce Canyon. These freshwater deposits probably covered the folded areas to such an extent that the Paria and most of its tributaries were developed on a relatively flat surface and incised their way into the bent strata after their courses had been determined.

Between Grosvenor Arch and Cottonwood Creek's confluence with the Paria River, the Cottonwood Cutoff road winds through Upper Jurassic sediments. On the west lies the folded crest of the Navajo Sandstone, plastered in several places with thin layers of red sandstone of the Carmel Formation. These strata are overlaid by the orange Entrada Formation, which in some places is nearly vertical. Atop the Entrada, usually on the eastern side of the valley, are thicker Winsor deposits, generally capped with resistant Dakota conglomerate. The Dakota is directly beneath the Tropic shale, which is protected by the Straight Cliffs.

For much of its length, Cottonwood Canyon is a prominent hogback. A horizon in the Dakota Formation near its crest is highly fossiliferous. The monocline was given its popular name, the Coxcomb, by Mormon pioneers.

Note: Separate locations have been designated for these activities.

Wonderful displays of wildflowers may be seen here in early summer, and the dunes contain a number of creatures uniquely adapted to this strange habitat. Most wait until cooler evening temperatures to emerge from the sand. Not far behind are coyotes, whose song can be heard puncturing the night silence.

The park has a resident park ranger and a campground with complete facilities (water is turned off in winter). A second campground, run by the Bureau of Land Management, is located on the north edge of the dunes. The state park may be reached via paved road from Highway 89 or, alternatively, from Highway 59 on the Arizona Strip by taking the Cane Beds turnoff and proceeding along a dirt road for about 16 miles.

DUCK CREEK

Elevation: 8,600 feet.

This sparkling little creek is only two miles long and is fed principally by underground waters from nearby Navajo Lake. These waters emerge in a big spring just east of the Duck Creek Ranger Station, off Highway 14, 28 miles from Cedar City. A short distance below the spring, the stream has been dammed to create Duck Lake.

In its short traverse over the lava-capped terrain, the stream drops about 400 feet. This rapid descent, coupled with the rugged nature of the streambed, produces a series of delightful, little waterfalls and relatively deep pools. Small trout, which are planted annually in this stream, provide excellent sport for large numbers of fly fishermen.

At its terminus, Duck Creek enters a pleasant meadow at the end of which it plunges

into the ground, presumably emerging again as springs at the headwaters of Asay Creek, a tributary of the Sevier River. Camping is available in a seasonal campground at Duck Lake.

Duck Creek Village sits in the large meadow at the end of the creek. This high country is popular among crosscountry skiers and snowmobilers in winter; a snowmobile race takes place here every February. Several inns, restaurants, tour operators, and essential services are available.

DUNCAN'S RETREAT

Elevation: 3,500 feet; population: 0.

Four miles east of Virgin and five miles west of Rockville, a few neglected fields, the remains of an irrigation ditch at the base of the hill, and a grave marker, placed beside the highway in 1940, are the lone reminders of a little village with the curious name of Duncan's Retreat.

Chapman Duncan and a few others first located here from Virgin City during the fateful wet winter of 1861–1862. In January, prolonged rains caused the Rio Virgin to burst its banks, with the result that the fertile bottomland the settlers had hoped to cultivate was washed out. Discouraged, the people moved away and sold their claims to new settlers. These newcomers managed to cultivate the typical Dixie crops of cotton, cane, corn, and wheat, as well as some tobacco, in 1862.

Local stories recount that Chapman Duncan "retreated to other parts of the country" after the Great Rain. Old settlers also said that Duncan "retreated" after having been ridiculed for surveying and building a ditch at Virgin City whose water would not run because Duncan had mistakenly surveyed the ditch uphill. A local wag wrote a song commemorating the event that went in part, "Way down south in Pocketville [Virgin], where Duncan dug his ditch uphill...." The new residents of the hamlet accordingly named their community Duncan's Retreat.

A post office was established here in 1863, and a log schoolhouse was built the following year. About a dozen families lived at Duncan's Retreat until 1866 when, because of the threat of the Blackhawk War, they were advised to seek safety in Virgin City. Despite this, however, the men continued to travel daily to Duncan's Retreat to cultivate approximately 80 acres, which resulted in excellent crops the following year.

Resettlement in 1868 increased the number of families living here to 14. However, the people continued to battle a series of floods on the Virgin River, resulting, by the turn of the century, in the complete desertion of the site.

ENOCH

Elevation: 5,500 feet; population: 1,947.

Thirteen miles southwest of Parowan, north of the road at a point where it abruptly descends a small hill, the slender spire of a church is visible. This structure marks the site of the little town of Enoch.

In 1849 Joel Hills Johnson, a member of the Parley P. Pratt exploratory group, discovered a beautiful meadow fed by nearby springs while searching for lost horses. Johnson claimed the land by right of discovery, and in 1850, when Brigham Young organized a party to settle at Parowan, Johnson eagerly volunteered. Johnson and his sons settled at the meadow in 1851, naming it Elkhorn Springs. Shortly afterwards, however, the name was changed to Johnson Settlement, and later Johnson Fort.

Although the Walker War caused the site to be abandoned temporarily in 1853, Johnson and others returned the following year and constructed a 100-square-yard fort. Three years later, some of the settlers were "called" by Brigham Young to assist in the colonization of nearby Summit. They accordingly sold their property to the Cedar Coop Cattle Company, a concern that used the lush meadowland to graze around a hundred head of dairy cows. While population declined during the next few years, between 1869 and 1870 new people came to establish homesteads. In 1876 authorities added a mail station. Two years later, a private concern built a foundry that cast stove grates, dog irons (andirons), gears, and other hardware.

The town received the name Enoch in 1884 when postal authorities protested the name Johnson because of conflict with another settlement by that name in Kane County (incidentally settled by the same family). The word Enoch applies to a city the Mormons believe was taken into heaven during Biblical times because of the goodness of its people and "there is reserved until the day of righteousness shall come." Enoch was also the son of Cain (Genesis 4:17) and the father of Methuselah (Genesis 5.21).

Farming once constituted the principal occupation here. The inadequate supply of water from the springs is supplemented by pump wells. In recent years, Enoch has expanded rapidly from an agricultural community to a primarily residential "bedroom" community of nearby Cedar City.

ENTERPRISE

Elevation: 5,300 feet; population: 936.

The little town of Enterprise is located just beyond Mountain Meadows on Highway 18, a few miles south of its junction with Highway 56. The history of the settlement begins in the ghost town of Hebron, on Schoal Creek, about seven miles to the west on Highway 120, which was named for a town in Israel and where a few settlers had been called in 1865 to raise cattle and engage in dairying.

Recognizing the limited opportunities at Hebron, Orson W. Huntsman studied the land where Shoal Creek left its canyon and ran north into the Escalante Desert. Here the amount of fertile land was virtually unlimited. Further study convinced him that the waters of Park Canyon Creek, a southern tributary, could be impounded in a narrow part of the canyon in Little Pine Valley. In June 1891, Huntsman engaged a surveyor at his own expense, and with a cost estimate in hand and the town site laid out, the encouraging name of Enterprise was selected.

By 1893, enough local interest had been generated that a company was organized and steps taken to start building a dam. Within two years, Enterprise's first family began construction of their log home. Although the project did not move rapidly, by the turn of the century several families from Hebron were migrating to the new town. The shortage of water often forced the colonizers to transport water for household use on horse-drawn sleds, which they called "lizards." No doubt the earthquake in Hebron in 1902, which damaged most of the homes, stimulated some people there to speed up their change of residence. By 1908, a hundred families had settled in the fledgling village, even though the dam was not completed until late October of the following year.

A second reservoir built below the first has increased the storage of surface waters and allowed Enterprise to expand. These waters are supplemented considerably by an underground supply pumped to the surface by electricity. During the summer, residents and visitors alike enjoy fishing on the reservoirs. Pine Park, west of the lakes, is an attractive camping area.

ESCALANTE

Elevation: 5,800 feet; population: 818.

The first recorded visit of a white man to the site of Escalante was August 27, 1866. At that time, Captain James Andrus and a party of militiamen passed through the area while en route from St. George to Green River on a mission related to the general Indian uprising of that year. The men cooked and ate wild potatoes found growing here and named the place Potato Valley.

Although Mormon missionary Jacob Hamblin passed this way in 1871 with supplies for Major John Wesley Powell's expeditionary parties, it was not until the next year that two of Powell's topographers returned to explore and describe the area. (They identified and named the Escalante River in honor of the Spanish Dominguez-Escalante expedition of 1776 that passed through here.) While there, Powell's men met explorers from Panguitch who were scouting for a town site. At the topographers' suggestion, the name Escalante was selected for the future town.

Encouraged by the amount of arable land, water, timber, and favorable grazing lands nearby, in June 1875 half a dozen men brought two wagons over the pass between the Table Cliffs and the Aquarius Plateau and descended a distance of 2,700 feet in 20 miles, rough-locking the wagon wheels in the steeper places. Living in

temporary shelters, they worked on their new settlement until December.

The following year, the present town site was selected, and the first families moved in. Land was divided, canals dug, and irrigation agriculture begun. Coal from nearby canyons furnished both fuel and some employment. The town grew consistently in population until the 1920s.

Agriculture, livestock, and lumbering remain Escalante's principal economic resources, although restaurants, motels and service stations now serve the needs of visitors. Highway 12 (now a designated Scenic Byway) was improved in the

The Escalante Monocline

The oldest rock in Escalante's immediate vicinity is the Navajo Sandstone, which folds upward to the north and northeast as part of the Escalante Monocline. To the south, west, and northwest, the Entrada Formation underlying the town rests beneath multicolored marine Jurassic beds, which are, themselves, overlain by drab grey to brown Cretaceous (chalklike) deposits. (See geology chart on page 23). The Winsor Formation found south and west of this area is replaced here by other sediments of equivalent age, including the world-famous Morrison Formation, in which the remains of a number of dinosaurs of northeastern Utah are buried.

Escalante Petrified Forest State Park has been set aside to protect the forest of "petrified" trees that has been exposed here by erosion. These trees were deposited in muddy flats 140 million years ago and entombed by sand and gravel of the Morrison Formation, thereby preventing decay. Over time, the woody cortex of the trees was replaced by crystals of silicon dioxide, which give the petrified rock its rainbow hues. A nature trail winds through the "forest."

early 1960s and solved the problem of isolation for the community. Increasing numbers of visitors now make the drive through the spectacular Escalante canyon country to Capitol Reef National Park.

The unpaved Hell's Backbone Road provides an alternative scenic route that skirts Box Death Hollow Wilderness Area from Escalante to Boulder. This route, over a narrow ridge, was used by mule teams to reach Boulder until the 1930s. Box Death Hollow Wilderness Area, managed by the Bureau of Land Management, may only be entered on foot. The quiet canyons cut by Escalante River and its many tributaries offer myriad hiking possibilities. Campers will enjoy the attractive high-country setting at Blue Spruce Campground. Nearby Posey Lake also provides good brook and rainbow trout fishing. The ruins, rock art, and artifacts left behind by the Anasazi and Fremont Indian civilizations, and now federally protected, may be glimpsed in a number of sheltered canyons.

Calf Creek Recreation Area, also managed by the Bureau of Land Management, is located in a canyon 15.5 miles east of Escalante on Scenic Byway 12. Here, a 5.5-mile roundtrip hike leads to a 126-foot waterfall, which is popular among bathers in warmer months. A campground is open between April and October.

FREDONIA, ARIZONA

Elevation: 4,900 feet; population: 1,207.

Fredonia is one of the few towns in that picturesque area of Arizona north of the Grand Canyon known as the Arizona Strip. Coined by an early Mormon leader from a contraction of the English word "Free" and the Spanish word "Doña" to signify a free woman, Fredonia is a fitting title for the little community. Since some of the early settlers were polygamists, a home in Fredonia provided comfort and protection from United States government officers in Utah and Arizona who attempted to enforce the antipolygamy law in the 1880s.

In 1884 a group from Kanab decided to build a reservoir on Kanab Creek about a mile below the present community. Even though there was no water in the streambed, they expected to catch enough of the early spring runoff to enable them to irrigate the land. They planted crops the first year but, because of the lack of water, none matured. The following year one family, who had built a house south of town, again attempted to raise a crop.

In 1886 floods removed the dam, and the presence of "a kind of Chintz bug" added to the settlers' woes by destroying their crops. Despite these problems, the people surveyed their town site and built another dam, this one on a solid rock foundation, which has allowed it to survive. The first houses were built here in 1887.

Fredonia has grown into a pleasant hamlet. For many years, its residents made a living raising livestock and doing a little farming. In recent years, however, the town's location at the junction of Highways 59 and 89 has led it to become a popular rest stop for travelers. A substantial part of the community's income is derived from a thriving lumber mill utilizing timber from the Kaibab Forest on the Grand Canyon's north rim. Fredonia is also the headquarters for the U.S. Forest Service's Kaibab Plateau unit.

From a stone lookout on the north face of the Kaibab Upwarp, just south of here, the vibrant rock formations that span the 225 million years of the Mesozoic and Cenozoic eras are spread out to view. Here, Nature has prepared a colored stratigraphic map contained in a Grand Staircase of terraces that rise as majestic walls to the north. In the foreground, at the base of the upwarp, rest the tops of the Chocolate Cliffs; above them, and beyond, tower the more impressive Vermilion Cliffs. Still farther north, the thick wall of White Cliffs may be seen—a conspicuous wall even from this distance. Although the broken slopes of the Grey Cliffs above these are largely concealed by vegetation, the Pink Cliffs, which rest on the distant horizon, form a conspicuous and fitting climax for this magnificent display of multicolored sedimentary rock.

GEORGETOWN

Elevation: 6,000 feet; population: 0.

In 1886 a few families located at Georgetown, a few miles south of Cannonville in the Paria Valley. By 1890, the 30 families who lived here were able to obtain a post office with semiweekly mail service. Eventually water shortages forced the colonizers to abandon their town.

GLEN CANYON NATIONAL RECREATION AREA, ARIZONA

Elevation: 4,300 feet.

The Paiute Indians called the Colorado River *pa-ha-weap*, meaning "water down deep in the earth," or "a long way down to water." It was Major John Wesley Powell who, in 1869, gave the 162-mile-long Glen Canyon its present name. Powell found the canyon's relatively placid waters and the pleasant glens of its tributaries a welcome respite from the wild and dangerous waters of Cataract Canyon, through which he had just piloted his flotilla of pioneer boats.

Lake Powell

Today, some of the area bordering Glen Canyon is Navajo Indian reservation land, but these canyons were once the home of Anasazi Indians, who farmed the fertile bottomlands, built dwellings in the sheltered walls, and left behind rock art. The waters of Lake Powell inundated the canyon in the 1960s, and as a consequence many archeological sites were consigned to a watery grave. But signs of the canyon's previous residents may still be found in the sheer rock walls of the side canyons.

Glen Canyon was first investigated as a possible dam site as early as 1921. Further study, in 1946 and thereafter, culminated in Congress authorizing the construction of a dam and powerhouse on April 11, 1956. About a year later, the prime contract was awarded to Merritt-Chapman and Scott of New York City in the amount of $107,955,122. The final cost of the dam, the powerplant, the switchyard, the new town of Page, and other associated facilities was $272 million.

By February 1959, the highest and second-largest steel arch bridge in the United States had been constructed above the 700-foot-deep chasm, south of the dam's surveyed location. Diversion tunnels and coffer dams to channel the river wat-

ers around the dam site were completed the following June, and the first of the 400,000 buckets of concrete needed to build the dam was poured.

The dam generated its first power on September 4, 1964 and was dedicated two years later by Mrs. Lyndon B. "Ladybird" Johnson. The Glen Canyon Storage Unit is an integral part of the Upper Colorado Storage Project, and the sale of electrical power has defrayed most of the total contruction cost. The eight generating units at Glen Canyon produce 1,288,000 kilowatts of electricity.

Glen Canyon Dam has created a huge lake that has become one of the most popular national recreation areas in the nation. When full, Lake Powell, contains 26,214,861 feet of water, covers an area of 161,390 acres, extends upstream 186 miles, and has a shoreline of unsurpassed beauty 1,960 miles long. Although the Bureau of Reclamation operates the dam, Glen Canyon National Recreation Area is administered by the National Park Service, which, together with the park's principal concessioner and the Navajo Nation, has spent $10 million in developing the five operating marinas, along with visitor facilities that include food service, lodging, boat and automotive repair, and campgrounds. The Carl Hayden Visitor Center, offering information, a bookshop, and tours of the dam, was dedicated in 1969. The John Wesley Powell Museum located in adjoining Page interprets the region through a variety of exhibits.

GLENDALE

Elevation: 5,800 feet; population: 282.

Two families named Berry and a few other families first settled Glendale in the spring of 1864, naming it Berryville. By the end of the year a dozen families had moved here, had built a water-powered flour mill using native grind stones, and had begun construction of a saw mill.

Geology of the Glen Canyon Area

The thick sedimentary layer into which the Glen Canyon Dam is braced is composed of Navajo Sandstone. This widespread, windblown deposit also covers most of Navajo Mountain, a place sacred to the Navajo (and also the Paiute Indians). Rainbow Bridge, another sacred site, is a natural bridge located in a side canyon close to Dangling Rope Marina on Lake Powell. It was gradually carved out of the entrenched meander of a tributary of the Colorado River by seasonal, silt-laden floodwaters.

Beneath Page, Arizona, and on a number of other slightly elevated areas nearby, the Navajo Sandstone is overlaid by a resistant layer of deep-red Carmel sandstone. North, east, and west of Page there are many buttes and mesas composed of this and younger Upper Jurassic sediments (Entrada and Winsor formations), many of them capped by the Cretaceous era Dakota Formation.

A few degrees northeast of the dam site, the great dome of Navajo Mountain rises to an elevation of 10,416 feet. The mountain is believed to be laccolithic, meaning that it was pushed up by an intrusion of magma through the thick, overlying sedimentary rock. In time, erosion reveals the igneous core material of laccoliths. Utah's Henry, LaSal, and Abajo mountains to the north are similarly composed.

The following year, Indian unrest associated with the Blackhawk War prompted the Berryville residents to erect a fort of log houses connected by a high stockade of posts. This enclosure, built at the site of the present chapel, covered two acres of ground. As added protection, settlers from Winsor (Mount Carmel) joined them and helped to erect the fort.

Misfortune befell the community in 1866. In January, renegade bands of Indians killed two settlers from Pipe Spring. Three months later, three members of the Berry family were murdered near Short Creek on their way home from visiting relatives. Church authorities advised the abandonment of outlying settlements, and in mid-June residents left the valley to look elsewhere for homes. That autumn, though, men returning to harvest their crops were ambushed, resulting in one of the settlers being wounded.

In 1871, a group composed mainly of politically displaced people from the Muddy Mission in Nevada resettled the village. Their leader renamed the settlement Glendale in memory of his birthplace in Scotland. Church leaders demanded that earlier settlers who did not wish to return give proper consideration to these new people. Here, as in Mount Carmel, the first year proved difficult, with grasshoppers destroying the first two plantings of grain. Corn from the third, which was nipped by frost and harvested before it was mature, did not make palatable food. Inadequate clothing made life even more uncomfortable.

In 1873 grasshoppers again took their toll on the harvest, further lowering the morale of the struggling community. As a consequence, when the Church instituted the United Order the following year, the residents agreed to try the experiment in socialist living; the order lasted only a year, though, before being declared a failure.

The economy of this little village has stabilized today. A thick seam of coal, discovered in 1891, is used locally and also exported to nearby communities. Ranching and agriculture form the main economic base. The local fruit is renowned for its excellent flavor. Glendale is located on Highway 89 and has several visitor facilities. The historic Smith Hotel at the end of the village, which for many years welcomed travelers, has recently been sold to new owners who intend to continue its tradition of fine hospitality.

GRAFTON

Elevation: 3,700 feet; population: 0.

Grafton, one of southern Utah's best-known and best-preserved ghost towns, lies seven miles south of the river along Smithsonian Butte Scenic Backroad, which turns south at Rockville, crosses the Virgin River, and continues either to the ghost town or over the mountains to Highway 59 on the Arizona Strip. The trip to this historic site is a must for anyone wanting to gain an insight into the 19th-century settlement of Utah.

The first Grafton town site, just a mile below the present one, was settled in 1859 by Nathan C. Tenny and others, who named their town after

Church, Grafton

one in Massachusetts. In autumn 1861 further settlers arrived, but that winter's Great Rain caused the Rio Virgin to overrun its banks, flooding the valley from "bluff to bluff." During the flood Tenny's wagon box, bearing Tenny's pregnant wife, had to be carried by wagon to higher ground. To commemorate the family's trip to safety, the child that was subsequently born in the wagon box was christened Marvelous Flood Tenny.

Because of the devastating effects of the deluge, which swept the valley almost clean of vegetation and incised a huge gully in its floor, the settlers moved their town to its present higher location, calling it—for a time—New Grafton. They again went to work, building ditches and dams and clearing sufficient land to raise a crop of corn and other cereal crops. Their optimism was short-lived, however; in succeeding years, the river washed out their dams so frequently that inhabitants jocularly remarked that "the making of dams and ditches was like washing clothes in a household: it had to be done every week."

In 1864 the territorial legislature created Kane County, and two years later designated Grafton as the first county seat. When the people moved to Rockville two years later to protect themselves from Indian unrest during the Blackhawk War, the county seat moved with them. Rockville continued as the county seat when the people of Grafton returned to their village in 1868.

Despite incessant problems in controling the river, the little town continued to grow until 1900, when about 120 people lived here. Thereafter, however, repeated loss of good farmland from flooding caused residents to move away, with many relocating to nearby Rockville. Today, descendants of the original Grafton families still care for the town site and work the fields.

Present-day Grafton consists of a little church, a schoolhouse, a store, and several wooden cabins—all in various stages of decay. In recent years, film makers have used the site for location work and have subtly "renovated" a few of the old buildings to suit their needs. *The Arizona Kid* and *Ramrod* were both filmed here, as well as the bicycle scene at the Rendezvous House in *Butch Cassidy and the Sundance Kid*. Worth a visit, too, is the old Grafton cemetery at the entrance to the village. Among those buried here are Robert Berry, his wife Isabella, and his brother Joseph, who were killed by Indians at Short Creek (Colorado City) on April 2, 1866, as they were returning to Berryville (Glendale) in Long Valley. The youthful age of those buried here is a vivid reminder of the toll exacted by this rugged frontier land.

Across the river, north of Grafton, Highway 9 traverses some interesting geology. In the dugway just east of the bridge, a heavy bed of conglomerate is visible lying in a trough in the brown sandstone rock of the Chocolate Cliffs. This gravel was deposited by the Rio Virgin, the same river that removed the chocolate-colored sandstone. More recent river deposits lie above those of ancient streams that flowed here during the Triassic period. The time interval between the two deposits is roughly 175 million years. These Virgin River deposits, known as the Parunuweap Formation, may be seen in several places along the stream.

On top of some nearby hills are layers of basalt, which originally came up through cracks in the earth's crust to flow over the terraces. Some of these lava flows look like they were deposited "yesterday," which in geological terms is true. Smithsonian Butte and Mount Kinewava are clearly visible from Grafton and Rockville. A trail in Zion National Park, north of Rockville, tra-

Hurricane Fault

The steep ledge on the east side of Interstate 15 between Cedar City and Anderson's Junction is the result of the uplift of a section of the earth's crust along a spectacular break known as the Hurricane Fault. The fault and the resulting cliffs may be seen to the southeast past La Verkin and Hurricane for 100 miles, continuing beyond the Colorado River.

The Hurricane Fault is about 170 miles long with vertical displacements ranging from 1,500 feet near the Colorado River to as much as 10,000 feet east of Kanarraville. During the same turbulent geological period approximately 65 million years ago that saw the building of the Rocky Mountains, the rocks in this region were distorted by folding. Subsequently, on at least three different occasions, they were broken by faults. The present topography is largely the result of the last of these movements, one of which is thought to have occurred within the last million years.

Just east of the turnoff for Zion National Park, along Highway 9, the road climbs the Hurricane Cliffs. A zone of movement (slickensides) is discernible in at least two places along the road near the top.

verses a petrified forest that was preserved in the local Chinle rock. Please remember that collecting specimens is not permitted in national parks.

GUNLOCK STATE PARK

Elevation: 3,600 feet.

Gunlock State Park, 16 miles northwest of St. George, consists of a 240-acre reservoir formed by a 117-foot dam, which traps the Santa Clara River bringing water to this arid area. The peaceful reservoir nestles amid red and grey hills, along the route of the Old Spanish Trail. The main attractions are fishing for bass and catfish, boating, swimming, hiking, birding, picnicking, and camping in an undeveloped area. A campground and a marina are under construction, and a golf course is planned.

The closest hamlet is the tiny community of Gunlock, named by George A. Smith for Jacob Hamblin's brother Bill "Gunlock" Hamblin, who settled a site of the same name near there in 1857. One story has it that Bill Hamblin earned his nickname because he kept the locks of the pioneers' guns in such good condition. Others say that the nickname was really "Gunshot" Hamblin

because Bill Hamblin was such a good shot. Hamblin was joined by another well-known Mormon pioneer, Dudley Leavitt, that same year, and subsequently by other members of Leavitt's family. The floods of 1862 washed out their cabins, forcing the families to relocate to the present site of Gunlock.

Today's residents, like their forebears, raise livestock and grow a few crops, with the help of water from the Baker Dam, which traps the Santa Clara River upstream from Veyo. The 50-acre Baker Dam Reservoir (elevation 5,000 feet) provides fishing for rainbow and brown trout, boating, hiking, and camping. The area is managed by the Bureau of Land Management. Developed and undeveloped campsites are available, along with a boat ramp.

HAMILTON'S FORT

Elevation: 5,650 feet.

When Peter Shirts, one of Parowan's original pioneers, found coal on Coal Creek in 1851, he asked permission of the Church to settle an area of fertile land on a small creek to the south. The stream thereafter became known as Shirts' Creek.

Apparently Shirts did not like living alone, for he offered to divide the available water with John Hamilton if he would join him. In 1852, Shirts settled by the creek and built a cabin there, followed a year later by Hamilton and his family. Hamilton and Shirts worked hard readying the land to bear crops, but in July they were forced to move to Cedar City on account of the Walker War. People called the site both Walker and Shirts' Fort.

In 1856, Hamilton and another settler returned and built an adobe fort south of the present site. Other colonizers arrived shortly thereafter, one of their number having purchased Peter Shirts's holding. For unknown reasons, the little village then became known as Sidon.

Church authorities advised, however, that the settlement be moved to a spot on the main road of travel between Cedar City and the communities to the south. By 1870, the inhabitants had constructed a new fort half a mile west of the present town. The 10 families living there named the new station Hamilton's Fort.

Because water in Shirts' Creek provides an inadequate amount of water for so many families, the population has declined. A few farmers still live here, however, and early pioneer homes may be seen on the north side of Interstate 15.

HARRISBURG

Elevation: 3,000 feet; population: 225.

In common with many communities in southern Utah's Land of Color, Harrisburg has had more than one location and name. Originally settled in 1859 at a point where the combined waters of the Quail and Cottonwood creeks join the Rio Virgin, the town was called Harrisville, in honor of Moses Harris, a Mormon pioneer from San

Bernardino, California. Before that site was abandoned, nine families had settled there. In 1861, the colonizers agreed to move to a spot near the junction of the creeks and to change the town's name to Harrisburg. There, they diverted the waters of Quail Creek to irrigate their fields, gardens, vineyards, and orchards.

Since Harrisburg was located on the road between Salt Lake City and California, a number of freighters made their homes there, contributing to the steady growth of the village. Despite being limited in size by the scanty amount of arable land, by 1868 the population had grown to 25 families.

When John Kemple, a prospector, discovered silver float in Quail Creek, in 1866, the townspeople foresaw a real boom. This did not materialize until 1875, however, when William Tecumseh Barbee found silver in sandstone just northwest of the town, leading to the development of the prosperous mining camp of Silver Reef. The temporary employment and market afforded by Silver Reef enabled Harrisburg to prosper, despite problems caused by insect depredations, floods, and the migration of many families

The remnants of Harrisburg

to Leeds—a village they established just to the north in the 1860s.

The combined effects of the move to Leeds and the ultimate decline of Silver Reef eventually took their toll. By 1892 only six families remained. Today, all that remains of old Harrisburg are the shells of several stone homes alongside Interstate 15. A modern trailer park now occupies part of the site of Harrisburg, surrounding the cemetery, adjacent to the recreational opportunities afforded by neighboring Quail Creek Lake State Park.

HATCH

Elevation: 7,000 feet; population: 103.

The settlement of Hatch, which lies just south of the junction of Highway 89 with Highway 12, came about in a somewhat opposite manner to other communities in southern Utah: it has gradually grown into a community, rather than having been planned. Whereas, other nearby towns with a larger initial population have gradually passed into oblivion, Hatch began as a ranch and has grown into a small, respectable village.

Hatch was named for its original pioneer, Meltair Hatch, who came here in 1872. Like many other Long Valley residents, Hatch was an exile from the Muddy Mission in Nevada. He first moved to Panguitch, which lies to the northwest, where he and others formed a cooperative cattle herd. Hatch and his sons first used this area to graze the herd, building a cabin beside the Sevier River about a mile south of the present town. As Hatch had two wives, his family was large enough to care for the herd, milk the cows, and process considerable amounts of butter and cheese.

Meanwhile, George D. Wilson had constructed a saw mill on Mammoth Creek, several miles above the ranch, where he used the running water to generate power. The purchase of this mill enabled Hatch to produce lumber for the steadily growing town. As Meltair's sons grew up, they also established homes, building on both sides of the Sevier River. In time, therefore, Hatch's Ranch became Hatch Town.

Mail service was slow to reach Hatch Town. Because Asay Town, a few miles south, had a much larger initial population, postal authorities established the first post office there. As this village declined they moved the post office to Hatch. By 1900 residents had built a small reservoir above the town. That year, however, the dam broke, and the released waters caused considerable damage to the homes below. Many of the early records of Asay and Hatch were lost in the flood.

Needing to find a new site, the people purchased land at the present location in 1902 and surveyed their new community. Although the post office moved along with them to the new town, for a number of years it continued to be known as the Asay Post Office. In 1906, the people received financial aid from the state to construct a larger dam. The new dam was designed to create a reservoir of 13,500 acre feet and to irrigate 6,000 acres of land, much of it in Panguitch Valley. Completed two years later, it lasted until 1914, when it also washed out. Even though this represented a loss of $178,000 to the state, the farmers down the river lost even more.

Farming and livestock raising remain important occupations in Hatch. A fish hatchery has also been built in what some might say is an appropriate location. A small number of visitor services may be found here.

HENRIEVILLE

Elevation: 6,000 feet; population: 163.

Between 1877 and 1878, families from the original town site of Clifton moved up Henrieville Creek in the Paria Valley, brought land "under ditch," and established Henrieville, so-named in honor of James Henrie, the presiding church authority who lived at Panguitch.

The first attempts at irrigation farming were discouraging: when farmers turned the water on to the land, a number of troublesome sink holes developed, meaning that some of the buildings had to be moved. Although the residents of Henrieville have had less trouble with their stream than have other valley residents, destructive floods have carried away considerable quantities of valuable land due to overgrazing of the range. Despite these losses, and the reduction in the number of livestock on surrounding ranges, agriculture and livestock raising still provide the principal means of subsistence for the people. Some residents obtain both seasonal and permanent employment at Bryce Canyon, with most commuting to and from their work.

Henrieville can be seen easily from high points along the Rainbow Point road and elsewhere in Bryce Canyon National Park.

The Virgin Anticline

This beautifully symmetrical, north-plunging anticline is believed to have been formed about 65 million years ago, around the time of the Laramide Orogeny that built the Rocky Mountains. At that time, these rocks were subjected to compressional forces operating from east and west in such a manner that the earth's crust was bent upward in a magnificent fold, or anticline. Subsequent erosion has torn away much of the dome, leaving prominent hogbacks on either side.

Three formations are visible in the middle of the structure, one composed of limestone—the Kaibab Formation; one made up mainly of chocolate-red shales—the Moenkopi Formation; and the third, which forms the flanks of the structure, consisting of sandstones and Shinarump Conglomerate, a member of the Chinle Formation. Less conspicuous strata include formations as young as the grey marine beds of Cretaceous age on the east face of Pine Valley Mountain. All Triassic- and Jurassic-era beds were also folded.

The nose of the anticline plunges into the ground just east of the north end of Leeds. South of Leeds, Interstate 15 parallels the anticline for about half its 18-mile length. East of Harrisburg, the waters from Cottonwood and Quail creeks have carved a beautiful water gap through the western flank and a second one through the eastern flank. Recently a dam has been built in the second gap, creating the 590-acre Quail Creek Reservoir, supported by a secondary dam to the south that crosses the anticline. The reservoir, when full, backs up through the first gap to the old Harrisburg town site. The upwarped strata of the Virgin Anticline are well displayed immediately north of Quail Lake.

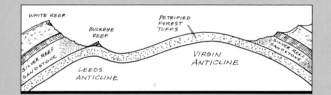

HILDALE

Elevation: 5,000 feet.

The new community of Hildale, on the Utah side of the state line separating Utah and Arizona, was created by the state of Utah to take advantage of the adjoining Arizona market. An industrial park provides work for a number of area residents. Adjoining Hildale on the Arizona side is Colorado City (Short Creek), a town that has figured prominently in southern Utah's Mormon history.

HILLSDALE

Elevation: 6,700 feet; population: 0.

The ghost town of Hillsdale in the Upper Sevier Valley was named for Joel Hills Johnson, who came here with George Deliverance Wilson in 1871 seeking a site to build a saw mill. Wilson, another recently displaced member of Nevada's Muddy Mission, lived temporarily in Panguitch while searching for a permanent residence.

With the arrival of two of Johnson's sons in 1872, the nucleus of a new town was formed, and the new village was surveyed in July. A rapid increase in the town's population in the 1870s, coupled with the desire of some residents to farm, resulted in a move to a new location about two miles up the river (to the south). Although some 30 families living there prospered for a number of years, in 1886 many became discouraged because of the shortage of irrigation water and moved away. At length only the Wilson family remained. They returned to the original town site at the mill and, as the lumbering activity declined, turned to farming and animal husbandry.

For years the only inhabitants of Hillsdale were the Wilsons. When George D. Wilson died, his brother W. P. Wilson moved here with his family. Despite this temporary increase the population steadily declined. Today there are no permanent residents.

HURRICANE

Elevation: 3,250 feet; population: 3,915.

The pleasant town of Hurricane is ideally located on Highway 9, 18 miles from St. George and 25 miles from Zion National Park, making it an excellent base for touring the area. The dramatic Hurricane Fault runs through the dark lava cliffs directly east of the town and is responsible for the volcanic features in the vicinity as well as the delightful hot springs that emerge in the Rio Virgin, between Hurricane and La Verkin, its immediate neighbor.

Without doubt, Hurricane is most famous for the story of the digging of its canal, which brought water from the Rio Virgin to the valley beneath the lava bench in 1905, and which led to the founding of the present town. With the recent construction of Quail Creek Dam to the west, water is no longer a problem for residents of the area, but the landmark Hurricane Canal is still easily visible, clinging precariously to the side of the great volcanic ledge towering above the town.

The idea of building a ditch at Hurricane was first investigated about 1863, when Erastus Snow, president of the Southern Utah Mission, took a surveyor with him from St. George to study the feasibility of using water from the Virgin River to irrigate new farmland. The topography of the area made the project seem impossible, and for a few years the idea was abandoned. Nevertheless, it was around that time that the ledge, and eventually the town site, received its name. While Snow and his companions were descending the steep hill above the present town, a whirlwind

Hurricane

removed the top of their buggy, prompting Snow to remark, "Well, that was a hurricane! We'll call this the Hurricane Hill."

By the 1890s, two problems faced the people in many of the towns along the upper reaches of the Rio Virgin: erosion caused by overgrazing of the top country by livestock was exacting its toll in disastrous annual floods that consistently reduced the amount of arable land in the lowlands; and the young people reaching maturity needed homes of their own, but there was insufficient irrigable farmland to go round.

In 1893, a committee was convened to reinvestigate the idea of digging a ditch at Hurricane. Their favorable report led to the formation of a stock company, which ruled that no man could own stock entitling him to more than 20 acres of land, except for those with mature sons who would also be given similar opportunities.

A survey indicated that to get the water high enough to irrigate the land, they would have to excavate a seven-mile-long canal from resistant limestone, much of it heavily impregnated with chert. Local labor would be contracted to build the canal, with each person paid for the amount he completed. Greater credit would be given for the more difficult sections, with adjustments to be made by the board when the original estimates were too low.

The work was challenging from the outset. The available tools were primitive, consisting of picks, shovels, handmade drills, crowbars, and wheelbarrows. In order to get the most out of their barely adequate equipment, one man, equipped with bellows and forge, was assigned to each camp to keep the steel implements sharpened and in good repair. Few of the workers, which included young boys, were skilled with explosives; as a consequence, several men were accidentally killed.

Ditch building generally took place over successive winters, allowing the men to continue farming without overburdening their wives and children. For the most part, workers lived in camps near the work sites and, until a wagon road could be constructed from near the dam to the canyon floor, they initially had to carry in their own supplies.

Today, it is difficult to appreciate the enormity and gruelling nature of the task the people set themselves. Lack of capital and good equipment forced the men to construct some sections atop unstable rock fills. They frequently had to excavate tunnels to avoid costly detours and, in some places, wooden flumes were necessary to carry water across tributary canyons. Furthermore, the builders were also occasionally ridiculed by doubting voices in the community. Despite their troubles, however, they remained optimistic, and, in 1896, to ensure that there would be no charges of favoritism, they surveyed the future town and drew lots for homesites.

As the ditch grew closer to the town site, problems increased. The hard basalt of the Hurricane Bench made the terrain increasingly unworkable. By 1902 the resources of the workers were completely exhausted. The board sent James Jepson, one of the members of the original committee, to the headquarters of the Mormon Church in Salt Lake City, with the result that the Church bought $5,000 of stock, providing a financial and psychological lift to the workers and allowing completion of the project. In August 1904, the triumphant ditch diggers turned the first water onto the arid bench. In 1906, 11 families moved onto their lands and, despite landslides above and below the ditch that made arduous and expensive repairs necessary, the little town grew until, by 1917, 100 families resided here.

Water here has worked miracles. Where black brush and creosote bush once grew, farmers now cultivate strawberries, apples, and numerous other varieties of fruit, leading to Hurricane's nickname: the Fruit Basket of southern Utah. Hurricane farmers also raise vegetables, grains, and alfalfa. What began as a harvest festival in 1914, evolved into an annual Peach Day, and eventually the Washington County Fair, which now takes place here every August.

Nevertheless, light industry and tourism are beginning to overtake agriculture in importance. Several small manufacturing companies produce unique items that are marketed worldwide; and a planned municipal golf course is further evidence of southern Utah's desire to develop recreational opportunities for retirees and visitors.

Despite the growing numbers of people traveling on Highway 9 between St. George and Zion National Park, Hurricane has remained unspoilt. The residents of this thriving, man-made oasis remain proud of their forebears and have erected two monuments commemorating the building of the canal and the town. One, an impressive structure made of native stone by the local Sons of Utah Pioneers, is topped by a bronze statue by sculptor George O. Cornish. It sits in the tranquil gardens in front of the Hurricane Pioneer Heritage Park and Museum in the town center. The museum (housed in the original 1936 building that contained the Carnegie Library and town offices) and the monument serve as a reminder of the 11 years of faith, determination, and hard work that made Hurricane a reality.

IVINS

Elevation: 3,050 feet; population: 1,630.

Ivins, located at the edge of Snow Canyon State Park in the shadow of towering Red Mountain, was named after Anthony W. Ivins, a local political and religious leader. In 1909, farmers working the land here began building an irrigation canal, after a survey two years earlier demonstrated the feasibility of such an undertaking on the Santa Clara bench. Although water became available for irrigating fields in 1914, it was soon evident that more land could be farmed if a reservoir could be built to serve the community. In 1918, the people selected a site atop the impervious multicolored Chinle shale and had a reservoir constructed within the year.

The first family settled in Ivins in 1922, and a post office was established two years later. Although the residents were plagued with floods (which removed dams and filled ditches), help arrived, in 1933, in the form of the Civilian Conservation Corps, a government-sponsored force, who brought these problems under control. In recent years, a larger dam, part of the Upper Colorado Storage Project, has allowed this small agricultural community to grow.

More recently, the National Institute of Fitness has built a residential facility between Ivins and Snow Canyon State Park. The fitness center, ideally located next to peaceful Snow

Canyon, provides guests with abundant opportunities to exercise, diet, and learn about a healthier lifestyle.

JOHNSON

Elevation: 5,100 feet; population: 0.

Before the white man came to claim its waters and to cultivate the land, a small band of Paiute Indians calling themselves the *pe-epa-s* claimed Johnson Creek. During a visit in early September 1870 by Mormon President Brigham Young and his party, John D. Lee noted that the company rode "down through a beautiful kannon [sic] clothed with grass like a meadow."

The following January, Brigham Young met the five Johnson Brothers in St. George, some of whom were there on a visit, and suggested that they "occupy the Spring Kanyon [sic] Ranch twelve miles north of Kanab, for a stock ranch." Later that month, Joel Hills, Benjamin Franklin, William Derby, George Washington, Joseph Ellis Johnson, and other members of the family investigated the area's prospects. All five brothers likewise played significant roles in Mormon history. Benjamin was at one time secretary to Joseph Smith, the founder of the Mormon Church. Joel, who helped establish a number of other southern Utah towns, was a poet who wrote the Mormon hymn *High on the Mountain Top.* Joseph was a gardener and pioneer publisher in St. George. William, after a decade in Johnson, moved to Mexico, and George was a colonizer of central Utah.

The family found "a beautiful kanyon [sic] from half to a mile wide, several miles long covered with grass, with small springs coming out at the foot of bluffs on each side, and a small beautiful stream running from the mouth of the kanyon

[sic], plenty of building rock, fencing timber, and fire wood, and plenty of excellent grass for meadow and stock range extending for many miles around." They made arrangements for a settlement and organized a cooperative stock association.

When William and Joel returned in March with the sons of some of the brothers, the whole family set to work plowing, planting grain, seeding gardens, setting out vineyards, and establishing fruit trees. By May, however, they were faced with a seasonal drought, which dried up their meadow land, and increased hostile relations with the Utes, Paiutes, and Navajos, who also used the area. At length, the ingenious colonizers beat the drought by excavating reservoirs next to the sandstone ledges where the springs were located. These long and narrow ponds enabled them to store water for irrigation during dry periods.

With the water problem apparently solved, the Johnsons were joined by a number of other settlers. For a time, the large building in which W. D. Johnson housed the post office and the Johnson Variety Store served as a place for religious services and other public gatherings. Sometime in the late 1880s, most public functions were moved to the new adobe schoolhouse.

About this time Johnson Canyon began to experience flooding, an inevitable consequence of the unrestricted grazing that characterized the early history of southern Utah. The floodwaters were sometimes so high that they entered the village. One of the later settlers reasoned that better drainage down the middle of the valley would solve the problem and plowed a deep furrow the length of the meadow to make this possible.

Although the floods continued to occur, the new ditch effectively diverted the waters and became wider and deeper at each high water. Soon it was obvious that there was a new prob-

lem: the valley on either side of the ditch was drying up, and it took increasingly more water to irrigate a decreasing amount of arable land. Nor could the water that was now seeping out of the bottom of the chasm be put to work.

By 1901 only a few families remained at Johnson. Today there are no permanent residents, although a few picturesque ranches are found beneath the bluffs along the valley's rim.

KANAB

Elevation: 4,900 feet; population: 3,289.

Many years before this town was settled, the site was used as a watering place and camping ground by the Paiute Indians who called it *Kanav* or "willows." Perhaps as early as 1858 white men came to this area to find feed for their livestock; and in 1864 Levi Savage, who grazed sheep nearby, built the first home here. That same year the territorial legislature created Kane County, naming it for Colonel Thomas L. Kane, a friend of the Mormon people.

In 1865, 15 families located on Kanab Creek, where they devoted the winter months to constructing a fort; however, the Blackhawk War forced them to abandon it the following year before it was completed. When some of the settlers returned in the winter of 1867–1868, they enlisted the aid of the local Paiutes in finishing work on their fort. In the meadowlands bordering the creek in Kanab Canyon, the men broke farmland. Some meadows produced such lush native grasses they were harvested for hay. Where there were no meadows, thick groves of huge boxelder trees and willows formed a natural wall.

When Brigham Young visited this outpost in March 1870, he was impressed enough with the area to recommend there be a substantial community here. On his return to Salt Lake City, therefore, he "called" a group of people with particular skills from nearby towns to strengthen the Kanab colony. They arrived in June, bringing the livestock with them that would form the main economic base for the town.

President Young returned in September and supervised the surveying of the town site. In that same year, Mormon missionary Jacob Hamblin achieved a difficult peace treaty with the Navajo Indians from across the Colorado River, who within a year had raided the area frequently, seizing an estimated million dollars worth of horses, cattle, and sheep from southern Utah settlers. During this visit Brother Brigham (as he was affectionately called) counseled the people to move their farms out of the canyon, and to cultivate the rich, deep, loam soil below the town—predicting that in time floods would destroy their canyon lands. Kanab Creek was then just a small stream, and pioneers tell of diverting its waters with dams made from a few willows. The men, accordingly, dug a ditch to carry the precious fluid into the village. Here, the people filled their barrels with water for domestic use during the early morning hours, as the ditch frequently ran dry before noon.

Believing that water was actually scarce, the townfolk were slow to heed Brigham Young's counsel, and for two more years they continued to farm in the canyon. An experimental crop of wheat planted south of town in 1871 grew well, resulting in a survey of these fields and their subsequent assignment on a lottery basis. With the abandonment of the canyon farms, the land was used as pasture, and the flocks and herds steadily increased. Soon, the animals were making their way into the side canyons and out onto the plateaus above the Vermilion Cliffs.

Kanab grew and prospered during this decade. The Deseret Telegraph Company's lines reached Kanab in 1871 and, the following year, Major John Wesley Powell made the town his headquarters for exploring the surrounding country. Powell's scientists, using solar observation and signals that came over the telegraph line, established an important baseline for accurate mapping operations. The United Order was introduced here by the Mormon Church in 1874, but was found by the people to be unsatisfactory and soon abandoned.

On January 1, 1883, Kanab became the county seat of Kane County. In July of that year Brigham Young's prediction about flood danger in the canyon proved correct. On two successive days deluges lowered the creek bed more than 40 feet, removing willows and trees and completely altering the topography of the canyon. As subsequent floods made the gorge wider and deeper, increasingly larger dams were needed to keep water on the land; however, the floods opened up new springs, and the water supply, when it could be diverted into their ditches, increased considerably.

Although the people of Kanab built a "permanent" dam across the canyon in 1890, in 1909 it too washed out. The following year, with the help of local labor and capital, the townspeople built the present dam, with a spillway and ingenious system of diversion tunnels. The dam provides the farmers with about five second feet of water for 1,800 acres of ground, the smallest amount for any irrigated district in Utah.

Supplemented by farming, coal mining, and lumbering, Kanab's principal source of income continues to be the livestock industry. In the 1920s, the surrounding dramatic scenery started to draw film makers, and more than 150 movies and TV series were filmed here. The colorful tablelands of the Vermilion Cliffs are particularly striking at Kanab and attract many visitors touring the national parks, state parks, and wilderness areas nearby. Several hotels, restaurants, a golf course, and other visitor services make Kanab a pleasant stop for travelers.

KANARRAVILLE

Elevation: 5,750 feet; population 228.

When the Mormons arrived here they found a clan of Paiute Indians under the able leadership of Chief Quan-ar. The Paiutes lived along a tributary of Ash Creek, which they called Kanarra Creek. The colonizers began using the Indian name for the stream and referred to the Paiute chief as Kanarra. They established Fort Harmony, the first settlement in this vicinity, farther downstream.

Before long, the settlers realized that substantial amounts of the water in the creek were either evaporating or sinking into the sand before reaching their irrigated fields at the fort. Consequently, in 1861, a few families left Harmony and moved to a place about a mile north of the present village along Kanarra Creek, where they built log cabins "string-town fashion." The residents of Kanarraville were joined by families from Toquerville, as well as about half of the residents of Fort Harmony, who abandoned their town in 1862.

The Blackhawk War, which caused the dissolution of a number of communities, helped to stabilize Kanarraville. A number of the displaced families from Long Valley (east of Zion National Park) came here. Because of the threat of Indian attack, these newcomers chose a site where the present schoolhouse stands and built dwellings "fort style." Older settlers moved into the fortress as Indian unrest worsened. Although the town was surveyed the same year, the lots did not begin to be occupied until the following season.

In addition to irrigation farming, early settlers found a ready market for beef in the mining towns of Nevada, encouraging them to raise a large number of cattle. Because rustlers also found Nevada markets, small owners banded together to form cooperative herds. One of these, the Kanarra Cattle Company, played an important role in the settlement of the towns in Paria Valley near Bryce Canyon National Park.

Located on the southern rim of the Great Basin, the water from Kanarra Creek can be readily controlled to run into the basin or into Ash Creek, and ultimately, via the Virgin and Colorado rivers, into the ocean. Today, a few people continue to farm, raise sheep, and a number "work out" in Cedar City. There are no visitor facilities at Kanarraville.

KODACHROME BASIN STATE PARK

Elevation: 5,800 feet.

Kodachrome Basin State Park lies about seven miles south of Cannonville on Scenic Byway 12 in the Paria Valley. The unusual name, which aptly describes the colorful rock spires found here, was suggested by members of a National Geographic Society expedition exploring the area in 1949. The park is memorable for its unusual rock formations, particularly the strange chimneys of greyish rock that loom incongruously high above the orange and orange-and-white layers of Entrada Sandstone in which they were once embedded.

Geologists studying the area have different theories about the origin of the chimneys. However, the most popular theory is that these spires, known locally as "sand pipes," may be the result of sediments pushed up long ago by water during seismic activity along faults in the rock. Millions of years later, when the soft surrounding Entrada Sandstone was weathered away, the more resistant rock was exposed.

The high desert park is popular with color photographers, who try to capture the shifting hues of the rocks, as well as with drivers, hikers, mountain bikers, and horseback riders. Overnight camping is available in a developed campground. A park ranger provides information and supplies at the Trail Head Station.

Visitors taking the paved Cottonwood Cutoff road from Cannonville to Kodachrome Basin will not want to miss Grosvenor Arch, a beautiful double arch located in Cottonwood Canyon, south of Kodachrome Basin. (Note: After passing the Kodachrome turnoff, the road continues unpaved to Highway 89.) The naturally occurring span of Grosvenor Arch is the result of differential erosion. The yellow sandstone that forms the bulk of the walls belongs to the Winsor Formation of Upper Jurassic age. The darker sandstone conglomerate that forms its crest is the Dakota Formation, which constitutes the basal Cretaceous sedimentary layer throughout southern Utah's Land of Color.

The larger of the arch's two openings is 99 feet across. Grosvenor Arch was also named by the National Geographic Society expedition in honor of Gilbert Grosvenor, president of the society.

LA VERKIN

Elevation: 3,300 feet; population: 1,771.

The idea of bringing water from the Rio Virgin onto the La Verkin bench was conceived as early as 1861 by mission president Erastus Snow. The project did not materialize at that time, however, because some people felt the cost would be prohibitive.

Kodachrome Basin State Park

In 1888, Thomas Judd and others considered carrying out the earlier proposal as a private business enterprise. By the following spring, after a preliminary investigation produced encouraging results, they had a working survey on paper. That June they incorporated as the La Verkin Fruit and Nursery Company and began business with a capital investment of $25,000. The object of the company was to "establish nursery orchards, vineyards, the manufacture of liquor, the promotion of fruit raising, stock raising and general farming."

Men employed on the project received $1.50 a day, half in company stock and half in "factory script," redeemable at the Cotton Factory at Washington or the Wooley, Lund, and Judd stores at St. George or Silver Reef. Since the ditch had to be blasted from resistant Kaibab limestone, construction generally proved difficult. On the brighter side, though, they made good use of dynamite, and the favorable Dixie climate enabled the men to work year round. In a few places they encountered gypsum, but this material was easily worked, and the completed ditch in these stretches looked particularly attractive.

At the mouth of Timpoweap Canyon they had to build a tunnel 840 feet long. Using a row of candles to keep their lines straight, the men worked toward the middle from both sides. When they met, their calculations were so accurate the ends fitted almost perfectly. During this phase, the abundance of gypsum helped the men along. Finally, in April 1891, they were able to turn the water onto the La Verkin bench, to set out seedlings, and to plant vines.

Within a short time, though, the easily worked gypsum, the presence of which had seemed so fortuitous earlier on, began causing trouble. Gypsum is readily soluble in water, and soon tiny cracks in the ditch became gaping holes through which the precious water escaped. Different solutions were sought, but each provided only temporary relief.

In 1895, leaders of the project decided to build a community and had the land surveyed for this purpose. Two years later, to meet unforseen expenses, they sold part of the stock and divided the property among the owners according to the amount of stock they still possessed. The landowners worked with enthusiasm and, when additional settlers arrived, the town received its name of La Verkin, after the creek that joins the Rio Virgin a short distance west. The name is apparently Spanish and dates from the early 1800s when traders used the Spanish Trail, which ran from New Mexico to California via this region. Some people believe that the Paiute Indians who lived here could not pronounce the Spanish word for the creek, La Virgin (pronounced La Verheen), leading to the corruption of the word as La Verkin.

For a time, the La Verkin farmers solved their leaking ditch problem the hard way: they took turns sleeping on the canal bank near the west end of the tunnel. When the water stopped running, the guard on duty would walk upstream until he found the leak and repair it. (To this day, the job of the watermaster is one of the most important jobs in the community, although problems now revolve more around water usage rights

than repair of the ditch.) The introduction of cement around 1910 gave the people of La Verkin their first real respite from leakage problems.

For years the residents hauled water to their homes in barrels or gathered it in cisterns. Then, between 1917 and 1918, cooperation with residents of neighboring Hurricane made it possible for both communities to share in the supply, which they piped in from springs near Toquerville.

By 1929, the owners of the canal had reached an agreement with Southern Utah Power Company to enlarge and cement the ditch so that part of the water could be used to operate a hydroelectric generator in the canyon south of the community. This agreement not only shifted the burden of delivering the water to the west end of the tunnel onto the power company but also made electricity available.

Today, dairy and turkey businesses have disappeared, and La Verkin is no longer an off-highway town. The community has spread westward across Highway 9 (originally built, about 50 years ago, through the fields as State Highway 17), to render the highway just another city street. La Verkin has been famous for its production of fruit, nuts, and molasses (Dixie Sorghum), but is now gaining prominence, along with most small towns in southern Utah, as a retirement community.

Year-round swimming and soaking are popular at Pah Tempe Hot Springs in Timpoweap Canyon. The springs have been used by generations of area residents, including the native Paiute population. La Verkin is smaller than adjacent Hurricane, which is better equipped with tourist facilities; however, several RV campgrounds are located close to the turnoff for Zion National Park.

LEEDS

Elevation: 2,750 feet; population: 254.

Leeds is the successor to its neighbor to the south, Harrisburg, which is now a ghost town. Because of some dissension among the settlers of Harrisburg in the late 1860s, some men decided to look for new home sites. Two and a half miles up Quail Creek lay Road Valley, which investigation proved would be a suitable place for a community and would allow residents to control the waters of the creek better. Convinced of this, Erastus Snow, president of the Southern Utah Mission, counseled those who wished to move to do so, but to make sure that water rights would be equitably shared by the two communities.

A family or two moved to the new town site in the fall of 1867 and spent the winter in tents. More people joined them in 1868, built dwellings, and named their place Bennington, in honor of Benjamin Stringham, their local church leader. In 1869, at Stringham's request, they changed the name to Leeds, after Leeds, England, where he had served as a missionary.

Discovery of the source of the silver in the sandstone at Silver Reef by William Tecumseh Barbee in 1875, and the consequent growth of this mining town a few miles to the west, brought prosperity to the residents of Leeds. With this ready market nearby for their produce, the town thrived for a number of years. Early apples and peaches sold for the fabulous price of five cents each. The residents also disposed of the potent Dixie wine at a good rate of exchange. Brigham Young spent most of his winters in the area. At Leeds he purchased land and provided a comfortable home for one of his wives. His son became the town's first village blacksmith.

With the decline of Silver Reef in the

1880s, an important market dwindled and eventually disappeared. Near the turn of the century a severe drought hit southern Utah, which further complicated the situation. Economic woes were alleviated in 1912 when Governor Spry sent convict labor to Dixie to build roads. The development of Interstate 15 has also been a blessing, since it and other new roads have sped up the transportation of produce to market.

Blessed with the longest growing season of any southern Utah settlement, the charming little village of Leeds still relies heavily on fruit production for its livelihood. For a while residents raised sugar beet seed and produced excellent molasses from sorghum cane; however, these items have all but disappeared now. A few residents own livestock, which graze on nearby ranges.

The Bureau of Land Management administers the Red Cliffs Recreation Site nearby. Here, Quail Creek runs through the middle of a campground/picnic area set amid red sandstone cliffs before heading east to Quail Creek Reservoir. Developed trails interpret the geology and natural history of the area.

MOCCASIN, ARIZONA

Elevation: 5,050 feet.

Moccasin is located on the Arizona Strip on Paiute Indian Reservation land close to Pipe Spring National Monument. The springs that rise along the Sevier Fault here were named *pa-at-spick-ine*, or "bubbling springs," by the Paiutes who have used the area for centuries. The more recent Anglo name of Moccasin was chosen by a settler named William B. Maxwell, sometime after he established his ranch on Short Creek in 1862, and prior to 1864 when he sold his claim on them to a Brother Rhodes for 80 head of sheep. On the day he found the springs, Maxwell had been preceded by a Paiute whose moccasined footprints were still plainly visible in the moist sand—hence the name "Moccasin."

Before Brother Rhodes left the area, he built the first cabin and interested Randolph Alexander in ranching there. By 1866, the Alexander Ranch was occupied by Alexander and his sons Murphy and Woodruff, and the latter's young wife Martha, a recent English convert to the Mormon Church. In early April, the Blackhawk War led to unfriendly relations with the Paiutes, and the three made a hasty retreat to the sanctuary of the family home in Washington, Utah. For a vivid account of this episode, read Karl Larson's *The Red Hills of November*, published by The Deseret News Press. Less fortunate members of the Berry family were killed during this uprising and along the same road the Alexanders traveled.

Moccasin Spring remained deserted until relations with the native population improved a couple of years later. Then, in 1870, the Winsor Stock Growers Association secured a third interest in the water rights, which within a decade were given to the Paiutes who make their home here. At about the same time, the balance of the water and most of the land became the property of Louis (Moccasin) Allen and his son-in-law Willis Webb, who turned it over to the United Order at Orderville, Utah, in 1875. The moderate climate at Moccasin was ideal for raising fruit, broom corn, and sorghum cane, and for several years, members of the United Order relied on the Moccasin molasses to sweeten all their food and used the broom corn to make brushes.

When the United Order failed, the ranch at Moccasin became the property of the Heaton family, who continued to live there and farm the land. In 1905 a school was built to serve the settlement. In 1907, the Kaibab Paiute Indian Reservation was established, with headquarters in Kaibab, about a mile away. The federal government constructed a schoolhouse, six rock homes for the Indians, and a residence for the superintendent who monitored Indian affairs. In 1909 Moccasin got its own post office.

After their school building was destroyed by fire, Paiute children joined with their white neighbors in attending Moccasin School. When one considers the clash between Mormon settlers and native people that led to the tragic murders nearby in the mid-1860s, the peaceful development at Moccasin stands out in sharp contrast to the turbulent history of the Short Creek area.

MOUNT CARMEL

Elevation: 5,200 feet; population: 150 (unofficial).

In the autumn of 1864, a single family came to the lower end of Long Valley, which is now bisected by Highway 89, and built a dugout about a mile below the present town of Mount Carmel. When additional families came the following year, some pastured their livestock in the area, while others began cultivating garden crops and grains.

Erastus Snow visited the settlement that summer. While he was there, the residents surveyed the town site and, at Snow's suggestion, named the place Winsor, in honor of Anson P. Winsor, the bishop of Grafton, who had religious jurisdiction over the Long Valley towns. (Winsor later built Pipe Spring on the Arizona Strip.) Only one family built at the new site that year.

Concerned about growing troubles from Navajo raiding parties, that fall the Long Valley settlers banded together for protection. The Winsor residents willingly joined with those of Berryville (now Glendale) and built a stockade at the older town. Although they abandoned their dugouts and moved their families to Berryville, they left their livestock behind, which necessitated daily journeys to care for the animals. The men took turns in guarding the livestock at night at the abandoned settlement. Although there were no serious conflicts with the native population that winter, problems did arise on several occasions between Indian raiding parties and those guarding the stock during the night.

The families returned to Winsor in the spring of 1866 to plant crops. Their stay was soon interrupted, however, by the outbreak of the Blackhawk War, which by June proved serious enough to cause all Long Valley residents to abandon their homes. For five years Winsor remained deserted, but with the abandoning of the Muddy Mission in 1871, the Church advised some of the exiles to reestablish the Long Valley towns, insisting that the original colonizers help the newcomers make a fresh start. On their arrival, the new settlers changed the name of the town to Mount Carmel, naming it after the town in Israel.

Many problems beset the residents during their first season back at Mount Carmel. Grasshopper depredation and frost caused several harvests to fail, forcing some settlers to supplement their diet with pigweed greens and other native plants. Lack of proper food, shelter, and clothing reduced the residents' resistance to disease, and an epidemic of measles that winter took an unusually heavy toll. But slowly conditions improved.

The Church organized the United Order in Mount Carmel in 1874. Since a strong minority opposed it from its inception, open dissension soon developed between members and their less willing neighbors. In the spring of 1875, members of the order resolved this difficulty by moving

upstream a few miles to establish the community of Orderville.

While the population of Mount Carmel may have declined in the past 30 years, it is still the home of a few stockmen and farmers. About two miles to the south is the junction of Highways 89 and 15. Mount Carmel Junction is a popular rest stop for visitors traveling between Bryce Canyon to the north, Zion Canyon just a few miles to the west, and the Grand Canyon to the south. A golf course and a small number of visitor services are available here.

Twelve miles southeast of the Mount Carmel Junction, the road passes three small lakes nestling in the bottom of Kanab Canyon. These lakes mark the base of the old desert Navajo Sandstone and occupy the same position as the springs in Zion Canyon. Below them rests a bed of impervious, deep red Kayenta shale, which stops the downward flow of the ground water and provides the water for the lakes.

Below the lakes and beneath the Kayenta Formation, the cross-bedded sandstones appear again, resulting in an interfingering of the windblown sandstone and the stream-deposited shale. The sandstone is quarried by blasting large tunnels in it; it is then shipped to northern Utah for industrial purposes.

NAVAJO LAKE

Elevation: 9,000 feet.

To the Paiute Indians who used this area, Navajo Lake was *pa-cu-ay*, or "cloud lake." Pioneers gave the lake its present name when they recovered stolen animals from marauding Navajo Indians who were camped there.

This beautiful body of water was impounded by the lava flow that fills the east end

Navajo Lake

of the valley, and over which Highway 14 is built. Fed by springs, but principally by melting snow and rain, the depth of the lake fluctuates considerably during the season. Before the government built the artificial dike to maintain a minimum depth, the waters of the lake often dropped so low that many fish perished during the autumn and early winter.

Water drains through sinkholes in the limestone underneath Navajo Lake, the majority of which have their openings east of the dike. This water emerges as springs that feed Cascade Falls, a tributary of the Rio Virgin (in the Pacific Ocean drainage), and Duck Creek and other tributaries of the Sevier River (in the Great Basin drainage).

The Utah Department of Natural Resources stocks the lake with trout annually, making Navajo Lake popular with fly fishermen. The U.S. Forest Service provides two excellent campgrounds close to the lake. Several lodges offer accommodations, meals, and boat rentals between Memorial Day and late September.

Between Navajo Lake and the Cedar Breaks Junction, on the north side of the road, a mass of black lava comes into view. These basaltic rocks, which are quite common on the summit of this plateau at Brian Head, are thought to represent volcanic eruptions during the recent Quaternary period. Geologist Dr. Herbert E. Gregory estimated that the youngest flows are no more than 1,000 years old, witnessed undoubtedly by local Paiutes (see "How Badger and Whistler got their Names" on page 10.)

The Cascade Falls National Recreation Trail (elevation 8,400 feet) may be found near here. Take the Navajo Lake turnoff from Highway 14, turn left after 0.3 mile, and continue three miles to the end of the gravel road. The water emerging from the high-walled tunnel at the waterfall and dashing wildly down the precipitous slope into the North Fork of the Rio Virgin is derived, at least in part, from Navajo Lake. Much of it enters the lake's underground channel through the limestone "sinks" below the dike.

The falls are not the only attraction here, however, since the 1.1-mile roundtrip trail leading to the cascades affords an excellent "upstairs" view of Zion National Park and an intimate picture of the Pink Cliffs of the Wasatch Formation from which the water emerges. In the autumn, as at Strawberry Point, the frost-nipped leaves of the aspen, maple, and oak add a breathtaking touch of multicolored magic to the scene.

NEW CLIFTON

Elevation: 6,000 feet; population: 0.

In 1876, around the same time as the Paria Valley town of Cannonville was settled, a few families settled in the east side of Tropic Valley, naming their settlement New Clifton, after the original town site of Clifton. Within a year or two, however, isolation and the lack of adequate water prompted the settlers to desert their town. About 1883, Isaac Losee and several others bought the property and resettled the outpost, renaming it Losee (or possibly Loseeville, accounts differ).

Even with the addition of water from tiny Pine Creek, which had been brought into the valley, the water supply was not sufficiently dependable to support the community. At length these families drifted away.

NEW HARMONY

Elevation: 5,300 feet; population 101.

New Harmony lies between Kanarraville and Pintura, about five miles west of Interstate 15. It was the first town to be established by the Mormons south of the rim of the Great Basin. The town was named for Harmony, Susquehanna County, Pennsylvania, one of the early centers of the L.D.S. Church.

In February 1852 a group led by John D. Lee, settled a short distance east of the bridge over Ash Creek, just north of the Black Ridge at what was later called Kelsey's Ranch. Because church leaders who visited the locality that spring did not think that there were enough farmlands to maintain a community large enough to meet their needs, they helped Lee and the others select a new site near the junction of Harmony and Kanarra creeks. Here, the settlers constructed an adobe fort 100 yards square.

The Walker War prompted temporary abandonment of the fort in 1853, but some settlers returned before the year's end. That autumn, church leaders chose Harmony as the headquarters for the Southern Indian Mission. Though some of the missionaries "called" to work with the Indians arrived as early as October, the balance did not come until May 1854. For reasons unknown, some of the new arrivals were dissatisfied with the location of the fort, resulting in the selection of a new site about four miles northwest of the original site. When Brigham Young arrived

later that month, he dug out a corner for the foundation of the proposed new fort. The people agreed to finance this structure with a levy of 40 percent on all taxable property.

In 1856, after receiving a petition from the settlers, the territorial legislature formed Washington County and selected Harmony as the county seat. John D. Lee was named probate judge, clerk, assessor, and collector. Until 1859 the second Harmony, or Fort Harmony, remained the political center of this new county.

The Great Rain marked the beginning of the end of Fort Harmony. With their adobe fort literally dissolving away, the people began to move up Harmony and Kanarra creeks to higher, safer ground. John D. Lee reputedly spent eight days and nights without taking off his wet clothes. Despite his efforts, two of his children were killed when part of the fort collapsed. By spring the place was deserted, and the former residents had begun work on a rock fort near the present town site. While the Paiutes called the new location se-ma-to, meaning "cove," the pioneers themselves dubbed it New Harmony. The first dwellings here were dugouts, but within a short time adobe homes had taken their place.

In 1866 the people of New Harmony surveyed their new town site. That year and the next, the Southern Division of the Utah Militia chose New Harmony as their training grounds for the Blackhawk War, contributing substantially to the early growth of the new town.

During the 1920s and 1930s the sheep and goat industry was successful in the region, but as was the case elsewhere in the vicinity, overdevelopment caused depletion of rangelands. Modern machinery in the late 1930s and early 1940s made it possible for many to turn to dryland farming, which continues today. With partial restoration of the range, some cattle raising has been reintroduced. Dairying continues to some degree, along with raising turkeys and chickens. These days, though, the little town is gaining in popularity as a retirement community.

People in New Harmony are blessed with a superb view of the magnificent finger canyons cut in the western edge of the Kolob Terrace of Zion National Park. These 2,000-foot, vermilion cliffs are quite inspirational, especially at sunset when the sinking sun makes the great ledges glow with an iridescence that defies description. Keen photographers will want to take a side trip from Interstate 15 to capture this view.

ORDERVILLE

Elevation: 5,250 feet; population: 422.

The tiny community of Orderville has one of the most fascinating histories of any settlement in southern Utah, for it was here that a group of devout and purposeful Mormon pioneers practiced, successfully for a time, some of the most exacting tenets that their creed and their leaders required of them.

Orderville was formed in 1874 as part of Brigham Young's experimental socialistic economic system and was known as the United Order of Enoch. Because it required the pooling of the resources of each for the good of all, the system was doomed to early failure in all communities where the people had been established long enough to accumulate individual fortunes. At nearby Mount Carmel, recently settled by the travel-worn exiles from the Muddy Mission, the idea found welcome ears. Although most of these people readily agreed to join the order, some families, led by earlier townsfolk who had returned to reclaim their lands, opposed the idea.

To quiet the dissension aroused by this disagreement, the devotees of the new scheme agreed to move up the valley some 2.5 miles and to found a new community, to which they gave the meaningful title—Orderville.

Early in the spring of 1875, therefore, they surveyed a block 30 yards square at this new town site. In its center they erected a 25- by 40-foot dining hall with attached kitchen and bakery. Until these facilities were partly destroyed by a flood in 1880, all members dined at a common table. Around this building they built rows of shanty-like dwellings. Since these filled as fast as they were completed, by year's end the little colony had a well-established, 25-family nucleus.

The principle of the United Order as understood by the Orderville community was, in brief, as follows: "That all the people are literally sons and daughters of God, that the earth is His and all that it contains, that He created it and its fulness especially for the use and benefit of His children, that all, provided they keep His commandments, are entitled to the blessings of the earth; that with proper regulation there is enough and to spare for all, that every person is simply a steward and not the owner of property that he has in charge, and that he is obliged to use it, and his time, strength, and talents for the good of all...."

To this end, each year they elected a board of directors to formulate policy. They, in turn, nominated an executive committee of "not less than three in number...(who)...when sustained by a two-thirds vote of the stockholders...(were authorized)...to take an oversight of all general business transactions of the company. Since a maxim was that "all things shall be done by common consent," all decisions affecting community members were brought before them in meetings held for that purpose.

Everyone who entered the system was obliged to deed his property, both real and personal, to the order. A board of three men made an appraisal of its value and issued shares of stock. They kept strict accounts of all transactions and made the books available for individual scrutiny by interested members.

All the men were given the same wage... "$1.50 per day for skilled or common labor, whether old or young. The boys from eleven to seventeen were credited with 75 cents a day. Women were credited 75 cents per day. Girls from ten to thirteen received a daily wage of 25 cents and those under ten 12 1/2 cents a day." The work day was long for everyone, with a bugle call sounding each morning at 5:00 A.M. to call all members to their respective tasks.

At the beginning of each year, everyone who had accumulated a surplus over what had been withdrawn signed a waiver as follows: "Orderville, Kane County, Utah, (date), I accept the above account as correct, up to date, and for the sum of one dollar lawful money of the United States, to me in hand acknowledged, do this day bargain, sell and transfer, to said Orderville United Order, the sum of (amount), the amount standing to my credit to the above account. This I do of my own free will and accord. In witness thereof I set my hand and seal." Those who were overdrawn in their accounts were released from their obligations.

Though the residents had to ration flour in 1876, in the years thereafter they accumulated more than enough of the necessities of pioneer life. Industries were consistently added within the town and elsewhere. A blacksmith shop, a carpenter shop, a sawmill, a tannery, a woolen factory, and a dairy were established in the valley. Mulberry trees were planted to nourish silk worms. At Moccasin Springs, Arizona, sugar cane was converted into molasses and broom straw tied into brooms. Some of the fruit was preserved in the molasses syrup. In Utah's Dixie, the Order bought land where they raised cotton and some early fruit. Their cattle and sheep, which increased annually, roamed the ranges as far away as the Kaibab Mountain on the north rim of the Grand Canyon. The Deseret Telegraph Company provided contact with the outside world. By 1882 Orderville was the most self-sufficient community in the entire territory. That year they inaugurated their latest industry, a woolen factory. The same year, however, saw the passing of the Edmunds Act by Congress, which prohibited polgamy in the territories and soon made refugees of many of the organization's most committed leaders.

It appears that a number of factors contributed to the dissolution of the United Order. One of the most significant seems to have been the inability of the young men to obtain stock in the organization. This stock was in the hands of the original members of the organization who had contributed their properties, and others who had entered the system after its inauguration. But since the books were cleared each year, no one within the system could obtain more shares, nor could those who had none obtain any. Furthermore, the value of the stock increased yearly. Of course, if the order had continued indefinitely, this would not have mattered, but in nearly every other town where it had been tried, it had been abandoned.

But there was another cause, which appears to be fully as important as the above, if not more so. As early as 1877, shortly before the death of Brigham Young, some church leaders questioned the wisdom of the plan. In 1883, with their stalwart president gone, a high Mormon authority informed the people that their system was not of divine origin, but that it was a "financial experiment." When subsequent investigation substantiated this, the people were deprived of their most important tie—one that had bound them together throughout all their previous trials.

With these and several minor problems facing them, the officers of the order turned to their church leaders for counsel. They were advised to try a new "stewardship" plan that would provide for varying rates of pay for different jobs and for the abandonment of the idea of clearing the slate at the year's end. Under this plan their problems multiplied rather than lessened, with selfishness and jealousy on the part of a few making matters miserable for everyone. At length the president of the Church advised the members of the United Order to disband.

In 1884, therefore, the residents of Orderville surveyed their town once more, drew for lots, and sold them at a top price of $70 each. The following year, they surveyed their fields and sold them to the stockholders submitting the highest bid. In 1889 the remaining stockholders bought the livestock and ranches, leaving only the woolen factory as company property, to be held until the expiration of their charter in 1900.

One could scarcely term the United Order at Orderville a failure, although this was the case elsewhere. Sharing good fortune or bad, as the Orderville residents did, calls forth the best in people. Throughout the years, the intimate spirit of cooperation, of give and take, provided for mutual security and community growth.

Orderville still depends upon agriculture and livestock raising for much of its income. Many families still grow much of their food in their gardens and orchards as did their pioneer ancestors. The proximity of the town to the three

Orderville

national parks has resulted in the construction of visitor services, which have provided added income for the residents. Those visitors interested in Orderville's past should stop by the small Daughters of the Utah Pioneers (DUP) Museum on the main street.

PAGE, ARIZONA

Elevation: 4,300 feet; population: 7,285.

Located atop the Manson Mesa, Page was established in 1957 to house personnel employed in the construction of the Glen Canyon Dam. It was also designed as a permanent city for government employees who would be employed at the dam and in the recreation area, and for those individuals who would provide services for both their fellow residents and for visitors. At the height of dam construction, Page had about 7,500 residents; the population is currently 7,285.

The community was named after the late John C. Page, commissioner of the Bureau of Reclamation from 1937 to 1943. Today, the town is a commercial center used by visitors and area residents alike.

PANGUITCH

Elevation: 6,600 feet; population: 1,444.

Panguitch is a Paiute word that means "big or heavy fish." In 1852, a group of pioneers from the newly established community of Parowan, on the western edge of the Markagunt Plateau, met a band of Paiutes belonging to the *pa-gu-its* or "fisherman" clan at Panguitch Lake. The Indians said that Panguitch Creek, which drains the lake, was a tributary of the *a-va-pa* (Sevier) River and that the two streams met in a broad, fertile valley. In July, a party left Parowan to explore the area. Although they found adequate land, water, and timber, they thought it might be too cold at this elevation to establish a permanent community here.

In March 1864, fearing that snowmelt from the previous winter would not provide adequate water for their irrigated lands, six families from Parowan and Beaver made the trek through Little Creek and Bear canyons, arriving at the confluence of Panguitch Creek and the Sevier River on March 15. Here, they found adequate water and land for a community, naming it first Fairview, then adopting the Indian name of Panguitch at a later date.

The pioneers spent the first summer breaking land, digging ditches, building stake and rider (rip gut) fences, and erecting suitable homes. An early frost nipped the wheat harvest, making it a poor first crop.

The first winter in Panguitch was so cold and the snow so deep that it was impossible to get horses across the mountains to Parowan. Consequently, some brave and hardy residents ventured into the mountains on skis, returning from Parowan with food strapped on their backs and on sleighs, thereby keeping the community alive. Boiled wheat and potatoes were substituted for bread until March, when the residents of Panguitch loaded some of the frozen wheat into a wagon, took it north, and traded it for flour. An adequate beef supply proved to be a real blessing.

By May 1865 the town had grown to 70 families. The new residents broke more land, built more fences, and erected homes. Although the following winter was not severe, deteriorating relations with the native people in the area, occasioned by the spread of the Blackhawk War southward, made it necessary for the settlers to be especially vigilant in guarding their animals against Indian raids. Across the river from Lowder Springs, eight miles north of the town, they erected Fort Sanford to safeguard travelers to and from Parowan.

In the spring of 1866, church and military leaders ordered a fort to be constructed in Panguitch itself. The resulting structure, which the people erected on the site of the present public school square, was large enough to hold 30 or 40 families. In April of that year, two skirmishes in the valley with bands of Indians increased the tension between the white settlers and American Indian groups to the point that authorities advised the settlers to move 30 miles north to Circleville. Although some people heeded this counsel, most of them went to Paragonah and Parowan, leaving their crops standing in the fields, to be harvested that fall.

Gradually, relations with the settlers' native neighbors improved and, on March 19, 1871, people from Harmony, Kanarraville, Parowan, and Paragonah resettled the town. They found the fort still standing and nothing disturbed. That spring, their numbers were strengthened by the influx of tax-

The Sevier Fault

For much of its 220-mile length the Sevier Fault parallels Highway 89. The ledges visible on the east side of the road between Panguitch and Mount Carmel Junction are the eroded edges of two lofty plateaus that have been uplifted from 800 to 2,000 feet along this great break in the earth's crust. The result of this break may be seen between Glendale and Orderville. Here, the east side of the road runs at the base of a cliff of red and white sandstone, while across the valley, to the west, the hills are a tan-gray color.

In two places highways have been built on the plateaus east of the Sevier Fault, following canyons cut by intermittent streams. The first, scenic Red Canyon, is traversed by Highway 12, the Scenic Byway that leads to Bryce Canyon National Park. This canyon is long enough, and the change in elevation so gradual, that one is scarcely aware of the climb through the lovely watermelon-pink limestone of the Wasatch Formation found along its entire length.

The second climb, just southeast of the Mount Carmel Junction on Highway 89 is more noticeable. This road cuts across several small faults in addition to the main fracture before it reaches the eroded summit of the Kanab Plateau. From the top, there is a splendid view of the White Cliffs rising to the north.

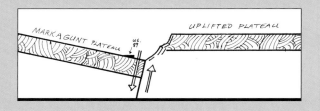

burdened people from the Muddy Mission in Nevada. Most of the families lived within the fort, but the following year some independent homes were constructed. Panguitch grew and prospered during the 1870s. Farmers broke land on both sides of the river, from which they diverted water for irrigation. Other enterprising men constructed lumber mills, shingle mills, and a flour mill.

Panguitch is located in the Panguitch Valley, at the top of present-day Highway 89, which runs southward through the Upper Sevier and Long valleys, forming a natural route for those people traveling to and from settlements in Arizona and New Mexico to the southeast. Because of this, the road through the town was kept busy with traffic. On March 9, 1882, the territorial legislature passed an act, creating Garfield County by taking a section from Iron County. The act also designated Panguitch as the county seat. The county was named for President James A. Garfield, the 20th president of the United States, who had just been assassinated. Panguitch continued to grow and prosper and was incorporated as a city on June 19, 1899.

The elevation at Panguitch, somewhat less than 7,000 feet, has given rise to jokes about the climate, resulting in an unjustified reputation. As a matter of fact, the summer climate is most pleasant and, even in winter, there are far more sunny days than cloudy ones. Nights are cool, but there are few days that remain below freezing. Killing frosts have occurred in the summer months, but they are rare. Cattle ranching still takes place here, but sheep farming has all but disappeared. In 1954, a modern sawmill was built, which still furnishes employment for many residents. Panguitch's proximity to Bryce Canyon and Cedar Breaks, as well as good high-country fishing and hunting, has made it a popular stopover.

Panguitch Lake, located on scenic Highway 143 about 16 miles southwest of Panguitch and 14 miles northeast of Cedar Breaks, draws many fishing and boating enthusiasts. The 1,250-acre reservoir is stocked with a good supply of rainbow trout and German browns. Three resorts on the lake variously offer cabins, campgrounds, a restaurant, a small store, boat rentals, and horseback riding between Memorial Day and Labor Day. The U.S. Forest Service also has three seasonal campgrounds nearby.

PARIA

Elevation: 4,700 feet; population: 0.

The name of this ghost town is an abbreviation of the longer name the Paiute Indians used to identify the nearby stream. They called it *paria,no-quint*, which means "elk river;" Paria alone means "elk."

In early January of 1863, Mormon missionary Jacob Hamblin and his party passed this way, having visited the Moqui (Hopi) Indians on the Arizona mesas. Hamblin made several trips along this route, crossing the Colorado River at the Ute Ford, better known as the Crossing of the Fathers (after the Dominguez-Escalante expedition).

By 1865 Peter Shirts, who was frequently in the forefront of Mormon exploration and colonization of southern Utah, had built a fortress in Rock House Valley about four miles below the present ghost town. Even though he and his family were affected by Indian unrest that winter, he apparently left reluctantly the following spring, when advised to do so by a company of local militia.

Brigham Young and his party visited the region in the autumn of 1870 and found that the Paiutes, with the assistance of missionaries, had grown some 35 to 40 acres of corn, turnips, and other crops. The following year over half

Paria

a dozen Mormon colonizers moved to Rock House, brought land under cultivation, and constructed dwellings and outbuildings. These settlers, and those who joined them in 1872, enjoyed a good harvest.

In 1873, Adairville was established a few miles downstream, near the spot where the Dominguez-Escalante expedition had crossed the Paria River. Before the end of the next year, however, trouble with their irrigation ditches caused the Rock House families to move to the colorful valley above the Coxcomb, where they established the town of Paria. By 1878 their neighbors from Adairville had joined them, since the water did not reach the farms situated below during the dry years.

With bounteous harvests from their farms and gardens and an increase in the number of cattle roaming the nearby ranges, the new village prospered for about six years. But in 1883 there were serious floods, followed by an unusually severe winter. Further flooding the following summer prompted more than half the 107 residents to move elsewhere. So destructive were the stream's swollen waters that only land protected by rock buttresses was usable for those residents who remained. Despite this serious setback, the surviving colonists were granted a post office on May 20, 1892.

Though doomed to eventual failure as an agricultural community, Paria enjoyed a short burst of increased activity between 1910 and 1913, when approximately 20 newcomers placer mined for gold. The gold was found in the chocolate-colored Moenkopi Formation, which makes up the peninsula on which the approach road to Paria descends, and in the Chinle Formation, which is seen in the predominantly purple-colored walls around the village. Since the gold only occurs as dust and excessively fine flakes, the mining operation proved unprofitable, and subsequent attempts to revive it have been unsuccessful.

With continued erosion from earlier overgrazing reducing the total amount of arable land to less than 60 acres, and mining activity at a standstill, Paria became a ghost town. A somewhat improved, though unsurfaced, road from Highway 89 was eventually constructed to accommodate film companies using the area (an abandoned movie set may be seen at Paria). The road is passable, except during wet weather. Some people think that the valley surrounding Paria offers one of southern Utah's most colorful panoramas. There are hiking opportunities aplenty in Paria Canyon, which is administered as a wilderness area by the Bureau of Land Management.

PAROWAN

Elevation: 6,000 feet; population: 1,873.

Someone has said, "Parowan is the mother of southern Utah." The title is entirely appropriate for several reasons. Founded in 1851, Parowan was the first attempt at colonization in the area by Mormon pioneers "called" by Church President Brigham Young to establish the Iron Mission in rugged, but resource-rich, southern Utah. Even

Rock church, Parowan

more significant, however, was the fact that so many of the town's early pioneers, having proved their merit in wresting homes from this wilderness, were subsequently called upon to lead in the colonization of at least a dozen other Mormon communities in Utah, Arizona, Nevada, and Wyoming.

In December 1850, a well-organized and fully equipped party of 168 men, women, and children left Fort Provo in northern Utah and made their way through snowstorms to the mouth of Center Creek (Parowan Creek), arriving there January 13, 1851. The little community was first dubbed the "Louisa Branch" of the Mormon Church, a name chosen to honor the first woman who entered into a polygamous, or plural, marriage. By January 17, the pioneers of the new town had elected officers. Two days later, these leaders met to lay plans for the construction of a meeting house and a compact fort that would serve as protection for the new community.

In May of that same year, Brigham Young and other church elders paid a visit to the settlement to see for themselves how colonization of the first area south of Provo, Utah, was going. The fledgling city was given the name Parowan, after a local Paiute Indian word meaning "mean" or "evil water" (probably a reference to the heavily saline body of water in the lower end of

the valley known as the Little Salt Lake). Parowan was granted a city charter before organization of the city was completed (an honor shared by only four other Utah cities) and immediately became the seat of Iron County. Rich deposits of iron ore in the mountains to the west had been discovered in 1849 by Parley Pratt's expedition to southern Utah, and the 100-mile-wide strip of land between the Rocky Mountains and the Sierra Nevada was duly christened Iron County.

By the end of 1851, the hardy colonists "called" to settle the area and mine the iron were becoming self-sufficient, with a saw mill, a shingle mill, a grist mill, and a threshing machine already in operation. This tight, little community built a council house, which served also as a social center and church, and on Christmas day dedicated a small schoolhouse.

By 1854 they had constructed a protective wooden fort around all the homes, the church, and the schoolhouse. Although, from the beginning, farming had been essential in order to provide food for the settlers, now shops for manufacturing and industry were also erected within the fort. Water from the canyon flowed inside through a wooden flume and served the following establishments: a cabinet shop, a tannery, a gun and machine shop, a blacksmith shop, a cotton factory, and a wooden tub and bucket factory. A harness shop, a shoe shop, a saddle shop, and a pottery factory were also built nearby. Some of the products of these early industries can still be found in Parowan homes.

Today, Parowan remains the seat of Iron County, and many inhabitants of this serene, little city still make a living in the same occupations as did their pioneer ancestors. Although a number of residents now work in Cedar City, farming and livestock raising continue to be the mainstays of the economy. The old art of ceramics was revived by the local high school, where students use high-quality, local clays to mold and fire attractive pots.

The residents of Parowan are proud of the important role their city played in the settling of southern Utah. This is most evident in the many brass plaques that have been erected in the town to commemorate the location of important early pioneer buildings. In the town center, dwarfed by county administrative buildings (including a Mormon Church building designed by one of Frank Lloyd Wright's students), the old Red Rock Church, built of dressed native sandstone and completed in 1870, still stands. This attractive building served as a religious and social center for the valley for many years. It has been renovated and now acts as a repository for many precious Mormon relics. Anyone interested in visiting this church, or any of the original adobe and log pioneer homes in the town, may do so by contacting the Daughters of the Utah Pioneers at the telephone numbers posted on the buildings.

Parowan is on Scenic Byway 143, which drops south after Brian Head to join Scenic Byway 14 near Cedar Breaks. The town's important role in the settling of southern Utah is reason enough to visit; but nowadays, many visitors stop at Parowan on their way up to the ski resort of Brian Head (14 miles away), or use the town as a quiet, less expensive alternative to Cedar City (18 miles southwest) for exploring the beautiful high country of the Markagunt Plateau. Ten and a half miles northwest of Parowan, at Parowan Gap, is an Anasazi Indian rock art site, which contains many fascinating petroglyphs apparently pecked into basaltic rock by game hunters 1,000 years ago or longer. Ask for directions in Parowan or at the Cedar City Chamber of Commerce.

PINE VALLEY

Elevation: 6,700 feet; population: approx. 300 summer residents.

Travelers in the area of St. George can hardly fail to note the lofty, snow-covered mountain range to the northwest. Pine Valley Mountain, named by settlers in the 1850s, was already known to the local Paiutes by two names: *kaib-a-harur*, meaning "mountain standing still," and *kaib-whit, kaib* meaning "mountain" and *whit* unknown. Several important rivers emerge from the Pine Mountain drainage, including Ash and Santa Clara creeks. To this day, inhabitants of southern Utah rely heavily on the seasonal runoff from these mountains to provide water for the region.

The first European to discover and name Pine Valley, which lies in the heart of the Pine Valley Mountains, was Isaac Riddle, who rode into its ponderosa pine–encircled meadows in the summer of 1855 in search of a cow that had strayed from the herd kept by the Santa Clara Indian Mission. Recognizing the wealth of saw timber there, Riddle spread the word to his friends and, by the following spring, the first of a number of lumber mills was constructed.

With the establishing of the Dixie Cotton Mission in 1861, and with mining activities in the Nevada towns to the west in full swing, southern Utah's lumbering industry grew rapidly. Lumber from the Pine Valley Mountains was even used in the construction of Salt Lake City's great tabernacle organ. The seclusion of Pine Valley, the absence of law officers, and the opportunities for work attracted, for a time, some men of dubious reputation. Those men who made trips to the valley for lumber from wine-producing towns like Toquerville and Pintura found a ready market in Pine Valley for their wine.

In 1868 Ebenezer Bryce, a former ship build-

er from Scotland who later settled Bryce Canyon, and for whom the national park was named, supervised construction of the Pine Valley church. Drawing on his nautical experience, Bryce fitted the handhewn timbers together with auger holes and wooden pins, constructing a sound building with an attractive arched ceiling that is still a masterpiece of craftsmanship. This picturesque church, the oldest in Utah still in regular use, continues to serve as an ecclesiastical and recreational center for summer residents and friends.

The 1880s witnessed a decline in the lumbering industry and a simultaneous increase in the use of nearby ranges for livestock raising. With no limits, for a time, on the amount of livestock a man could own, the area where they could be fed, or the length of the grazing season, the income from ranching was for a number of years considerable. In the meantime, dairying had also proven to be practical, as well as the raising of grain, alfalfa, and potatoes.

During the early 1930s, the federally funded Civilian Conservation Corps established a camp

Chapel, Pine Valley

in the area. They improved roads, built a reservoir, and constructed a spacious public campground that is now part of Pine Valley Recreation Area. The reservoir and the Santa Clara River were stocked with brook and rainbow trout. In summer, the Pine Valley Recreation Area, located just a few miles beyond Pine Valley, is a favorite destination for picnickers, fishermen, hikers, backpackers, campers, and anyone wishing to escape the sizzling temperatures of the lower elevations. In winter, ample snowfall provides good crosscountry skiing along trails throughout Dixie National Forest. The 50,000-acre Pine Valley Wilderness, administered by the U.S. Forest Service, offers hikers and horseback riders terrific views and a network of long hiking trails throughout the mountains.

PINTO

Elevation: 6,050 feet; population: some summer residents only.

This little settlement on Pinto Creek probably received its name from the variety of colors in the nearby hills. Since it served as a favored camping site on the Old Spanish Trail, it was well known to white explorers before the arrival of the Mormons.

As early as 1865, Indian missionaries found that forage had been harvested at Pinto as hay. Perhaps this proven agricultural potential led them to settle here shortly thereafter. Within six years a rock chapel had been erected. By 1871, the original a half dozen families had grown to 14.

During the town's approximate 50 years of existence, the residents of Pinto raised livestock and produced dairy products successfully. In 1916, however, some families began to move to Newcastle a few miles to the north, where more arable land was available. Although two families remained until the 1930s, there are no permanent residents there today.

The Pine Valley Mountians

The Pine Valley Mountains, whose top peak rises 10,324 feet above sea level, is made up of more than 3,000 feet of semicrystalline material (latite-porphyry) that once was molten lava. This igneous material pushed up through thick layers of sedimentary rock millions of years ago. Erosion of the overlying sedimentary strata has now revealed the laccolithic core of the Pine Valley Mountains.

Of the many sedimentary layers still visible, the youngest are brightly colored freshwater limestones and marl from the Wasatch Formation, which constitute the same reddish strata so vividly displayed at Cedar Breaks National Monument and Bryce Canyon National Park. The grey Cretaceous rocks underneath these layers were formed from sands, clays, and limes deposited by streams along the shore of the last great ocean covering this land.

PINTURA

Elevation: 4,000 feet; population 14 (unofficial).

Just north of the Toquerville exit, along Interstate 15, are several almost-deserted hamlets on the old thoroughfare, now bypassed by the busy interstate. What remains of the pretty, little village of Pintura is found here, its weathered wooden buildings and orchards a startling contrast to the steep banks of the Black Ridge towering above it.

Pintura, which was originally called Ashton, then Bellevue, before its final incarnation as Pintura, lies on the right bank of Ash Creek and was used as a ranch, perhaps as early as 1858. At that time, early pioneers were clearing land and excavating ditches in order to control the meager water supply emerging from the Pine Valley Mountain drainage to the northwest. From the comfort of the interstate, it is hard to imagine

the difficulty the steep lava bench of Black Ridge once caused for travelers in southern Utah. The building of a road here in 1862 opened up communications and allowed settlement in an area once cut off by the impassable lava.

From the beginning, Washington County officials recognized that a road would have to be built through this area; therefore, in December 1856, the "selectmen" appointed Peter Shirts as road commissioner and appropriated $300 for the road's construction. Even though Shirts was able to build the road over the top of the ridge, on the south end he found it impossible to locate a place where wagons could be taken down the ridge in one piece. Consequently, at "Peter's Leap" travelers dismantled their vehicles and took them down in sections.

In 1862, Erastus Snow asked the people in Cedar City and Harmony to build a new road. The road you see today from the interstate, which follows Ash Creek at the base of the Black Ridge, was their narrow but passable route. With its completion in 1863, new colonizers arrived at the ranch and named their tiny hamlet Ashton. Three years later, discouraged by the lack of perennial water, the original settler sold his improvements to Joel H. Johnson, a pioneer of Parowan, and the founder of Enoch. By the next year, however, the Blackhawk War had forced abandonment.

When the town was resettled in 1868, a number of new families moved in. Viewing the picturesque little valley from the Black Ridge, they observed its bell-shaped contour and called it Bellvue. Written Bellevue, this title was retained until 1925, when postal authorities requested a change. Residents chose the name Pintura, a Spanish word meaning "picture" or "painting."

As Bellevue was just a good day's drive from Cedar City and many of the Dixie settlements, it soon became the traveler's "Great Camp Ground." During the boom days of the mining town of Silver Reef, it was not unusual to find 200 or more wagons on the road daily. With the great barn at Bellevue often overflowing with draft animals, many were staked outside. Three camp houses gave teamsters respite from the frigid, wintry blasts that came howling over the Black Ridge. At length, residents constructed a cement cistern to store the cool, clear water, abundant in the springtime, for use in the hot, dry summer months.

Johnson imported choice Muscat, Concord, and California grape roots, some from France. When their fruits ripened, residents carefully pressed and cultured them to produce popular, high-quality wines. Until Congress and the people passed the 18th amendment, wine making remained an important industry in Bellevue.

The orchards that replaced the vineyards, and thriving vegetable gardens, continue to feed the few remaining residents, as well as providing a surplus for sale. Livestock pastured on the nearby ranges also supplement the income.

PIPE SPRING NATIONAL MONUMENT, ARIZONA

Elevation: 5,000 feet.

For untold centuries, the springs that gush up along the Sevier Fault at Pipe Spring have provided a reliable water source for travelers in the area north of the Grand Canyon known as the Arizona Strip. The earliest people to use the springs were native people, who wandered far and wide in this desert. In the beginning, paleo-Indian hunters probably stopped by the natural spring, followed, around the time of Christ, by nomadic hunter-gatherer Anasazi Indians, and later by peripatetic Paiutes. Then, in the 19th

The Black Ridge

To date no one has been able to determine just when the heavy black basaltic lava of the Black Ridge was ejected as molten rock. Authorities agree, however, that it must have been within the last million years, and that at least part of it was extruded before the last movement along the Hurricane Fault. In other words, the black rock found atop the cliffs, and that located beneath Interstate 15 at the base of the ledge, formed a continuous sheet of lava until the last vertical movement along the Hurricane Fault tore the two sections apart and elevated the eastern one to its present lofty position.

A feature of special interest here is the manner in which the lava on the Black Ridge is bent downward toward Ash Creek along the base of the fault. Not only is the lava so affected, but the layers beneath it are similarly downwarped. This may be due, at least in part, to the movement of large masses of molten lava from underground and their extrusion onto the surface of the land prior to the periods of downwarping. The crust is believed to have slumped to fill the void created by the loss of the lava. This unusual phenomena and others associated with it have prompted more exhaustive study, which may result in new conclusions.

century, the springs came to be important to white men settling the western frontier.

Though we don't know what the native people called it, Pipe Spring received its Anglo name in 1856 when the first white travelers to discover it camped here for the night while journeying to the Hopi Mesas to the southeast. A member of the party, which was led by Mormon missionary Jacob Hamblin, tricked Jacob's brother, "Gunlock Bill" Hamblin, into trying to shoot a hole in a silk handkerchief, which he had hung by one end. Despite his reputation as an excellent marksman, Gunlock Bill apparently was unaware that the bullet would not penetrate the silk regardless of how well it was aimed. Exasperated at his failure, Gunlock Bill wagered he could shoot the bottom out of a pipe at 50 paces without touching the bowl. When he won the bet, the men christened the place Pipe Spring.

The first settlers at Pipe Spring were Dr. James M. Whitmore, Robert McIntire, and

Whitmore's young son. The three built a primitive dugout shelter here in 1863 and ran a cattle ranch. During the winter of 1866, however, the two older men were killed while trying to get back stolen livestock from a group of Indians who had raided the ranch. Whitmore's young son raised the alarm when the men did not return, and a posse set out after them, finding their bodies in the snow a distance from Pipe Spring. Although several Paiutes found with the dead men's effects were executed on the spot by the angry posse, exactly which native group carried out the murders remains a mystery. Current opinion maintains that the raiders were made up of renegade Paiutes working alongside disgruntled Navajos who were crossing the Colorado River in order to raid livestock on the Arizona Strip.

Anger was running high among the Mormon community when, three months later, a few miles northwest of the spring, another group of Indians surprised and murdered John and Robert

Winsor Castle, Pipe Spring National Monument

Berry and Robert's young wife near Short Creek (Colorado City), as they were returning to their homes in Berryville (Glendale). Raiding continued for a number of years, with Jacob Hamblin and others attempting to negotiate peace between the white settlers and the native groups throughout the 1870s with varying degrees of success. Not until the end of the century, was a lasting peace eventually worked out between the Utes, the Navajo, and their Paiute allies in the San Juan area, which brought the situation under control.

Brigham Young decided to acquire Pipe Spring for the Mormon Church in 1869, believing that the spring's good location would serve the local Mormon communities well. He "called" the bishop of Grafton, Anson P. Winsor, and his family to Pipe Spring and directed him to construct a fort, part of which would enclose the spring, thereby keeping it safe for Mormon use. The fort (known as Winsor Castle in a reference to Winsor's British heritage) was completed the following year. It served, for a number of years, as the headquarters for the Church's large herd of cattle, which were given by many Mormons as their annual tithing payment. By the winter of 1871 communication with the rest of the world

was made possible by the installation of the Deseret Telegraph Line. Major John Wesley Powell stayed here several times during his landmark explorations of the Grand Canyon region. In 1870, he and Jacob Hamblin negotiated an important peace settlement between the Mormons and the Navajos.

During the 1870s, the dairy operation at Pipe Spring provided an abundant and important supply of meat, cheese, and other dairy products for the construction workers erecting the St. George Temple to the west. Later, following completion of the temple in 1877 and as ranching operations at Pipe Spring began to decline, the fort became popular as a rest stop for couples going to the temple to be "sealed" in marriage. In the 1880s, Pipe Spring's thick walls also sheltered polygamists fleeing prosecution under the government's antipolygamy laws. By 1888, Pipe Spring had been sold to a non-Mormon rancher, but overgrazing had irreparably stressed the range, and Pipe Spring's days as a cattle ranch were numbered.

The historic Pipe Spring ranch was eventually sold to the National Park Service. It was set aside as Pipe Spring National Monument in 1923 to serve as a reminder of the vital role the springs have played in the lives of native people and in the development of ranching in the West. A visitor center provides information about the monument, and guided tours of the site are offered throughout the day. Visitors see the original, restored, two-story fort and many pioneer artifacts commemorating ranch life. Longhorn cattle are corralled in pens alongside the workshops that were essential to self-sufficiency.

The construction of Highway 59 south of the Vermilion Cliffs from Fredonia, Arizona, to Hurricane, Utah, in the 1960s did a great deal to make this little national park unit accessible.

Today, it is a popular stopping point for travelers en route to St. George or to nearby Zion National Park. The Paiute tribe, whose reservation surrounds Pipe Spring, runs a small campground across from the monument; a cafeteria at the monument provides authentic western fare.

QUAIL CREEK RESERVOIR

Elevation: 3,400 feet.

Quail Creek Reservoir, completed in 1985, is the culmination of many decades of study and political maneuvering. The original proposal, which called for a dam in the Virgin River above the Hurricane Fault, was abandoned when caverns were discovered in the limestone subsurface. Over the years, several alternative sites were considered; in 1985, construction began at the present off-stream location.

The project involved much more than one dam. The most obvious structure is a 2,000-foot-long-dike, or secondary dam, built on the eroded floor of the Virgin Anticline and clearly visible from Highway 9. The main dam is much less conspicuous, being anchored into the stable Shinarump Conglomerate in a narrow gap of the

Quail Creek Reservoir

anticline's east limb.

Quail Creek supplies only a small amount of the volume of water (40,000 acre feet) required to fill the lake, the principal source being the Virgin River. From a third dam, nearly nine miles upstream, a penstock pipeline, varying in size from 48 inches to 66 inches, supplies irrigation water to La Verkin and Hurricane, retiring the upper ends of the historic canals that supplied those towns. It then passes through a new 2,340-kilowatt hydropower plant before discharging into the reservoir.

Trouble in the form of leaks under the dike began showing up before the lake had filled. Soluble gypsum and other unstable minerals failed to support the dike, which collapsed simultaneously with the coming of the New Year 1989. The collapse released 25,000 acre feet of water within an hour, causing much damage to roads, bridges, farms, and homes below. Fortunately, no lives were lost.

A new concrete dike, with a foundation 50 feet below ground, replaced the damaged one and, by late spring 1991, the reservoir was again full. In addition to providing a prime recreational facility—boating, fishing, swimming—the lake is an added source of culinary water for St. George and vicinity, with the addition of a new purification plant.

ROCKVILLE

Elevation: 3,750 feet; population: 182.

One of the first towns to be established in the Virgin River Valley immediately west of present-day Zion National Park was formed in the autumn of 1861, when part of the group "called" to settle Utah's Dixie left the main body at the junction of La Verkin Creek and the Rio Virgin to occupy sites "up the river." Arriving at a spot about a half

Autumn in the Virgin River valley west of Rockville

mile below the present town, they built a few dugouts and crude huts and christened the remote outpost "Adventure."

The Great Rain that winter convinced the colonizers that they had built too close to the river. As a consequence, the following spring they agreed to move up the river to the present location, which they promptly surveyed and named Rockville because of the many boulders on the nearby hills.

Though they did not move to Rockville until November, before the winter was over a dozen families had established residence here. Since the settlers arrived too late to plant crops, they spent most of their time breaking land, digging ditches, building fences, constructing dugouts, and erecting log houses. As the next year's harvest was a long way away, some men had to leave their work for a time and go north to obtain food to feed their families.

The Church encouraged the settlers to plant cotton, corn, cane, and a little wheat. In anticipation of a cane harvest, the residents of Rockville built a crusher or sorghum mill, using rollers cast from iron produced at Cedar City. Due to inadequate fencing, the young people were required to keep the livestock out of the fields.

In 1866 the Blackhawk War, which caused the abandonment of Shunesburg, Springdale, and Grafton, raised the population of Rockville to about 200 souls. When the residents of Grafton, the seat of Kane County, arrived, the county seat was transfered to Rockville along with them, and here it remained until an act of the territorial legislature on February 19, 1869, moved it to "Tokerville."

Within a few years the Rockville residents had introduced fruit into the village and replaced cotton with grains and garden crops to ensure adequate food for their families. The last export crop of cotton was cultivated in 1870. Some of the present residents of this attractive village still produce fruit and garden crops for their own consumption. Strawberries are harvested in June, and throughout the summer months other fresh fruits are picked. Some of this produce finds a ready market among locals and travelers on Highway 9 to Zion National Park. The nearby ranges provide forage for livestock. A few families derive all or part of their income from employment in Zion National Park. The pleasant Smithsonian Butte Scenic Backroad crosses the river at Rockville and leads to the ghost town of Grafton and on over the mountains to Highway 59 on the Arizona Strip.

ST. GEORGE

Elevation: 2,900 feet; population: 28,502.

St. George is today the largest of all the towns founded as part of the Cotton Mission of 1861 and the fastest-growing city in Utah. A combination of factors is responsible, among them the fact that most of the original company of 309 families who were "called" settled here, and in recent years, the mild climate and abundant recreational opportunities have made St. George an attractive retirement center.

When the colonizers arrived early in December 1861, they made a temporary camp about half a mile east of the present Mormon temple, at the site of the present Dixie College campus. Here they remained until they surveyed their city and drew for their lots. St. George was named in honor of Mormon apostle George A. Smith who, although he did not participate in the town's settlement, had personally selected most of the company and was generally known as the "father of the Southern Utah missions."

The first year in the new community was very difficult. The Great Rain that winter caused

St. George

considerable discomfort; forage for livestock was scarce; the water available for household use contained so much alkali that it could hardly be used; and the heat during the summer months, while not dangerous, was far from pleasant. Floods along the Rio Virgin, the story of which is told in connection with the settlement of Washington, further complicated their problems.

It soon became obvious to Brigham Young

in Salt Lake City that the pioneers would need assistance. Although the group had been carefully selected by their leaders as the ones best qualified to colonize the area, even the efforts of the best of men may prove futile in the face of Nature's wrath. To boost the spirits of the demoralized group, President Young sent a letter to Erastus Snow, president of the Southern Utah Mission, in October 1862, requesting the construction of a meeting house "large enough to comfortably seat at least a thousand persons and that will not only be useful, but also an ornament to your city and a credit to your enterprise." All of the tithing of St. George, Cedar City, and the towns of southern Utah was to be used for this purpose. On June 1, 1863, the St. George pioneers began construction of their New England–style tabernacle.

Since the tabernacle, and later the temple, were financed by tithing, a word of explanation is in order. Faithful Mormons, of their own volition, pay a tenth of their annual profits to their church. Because money was scarce in the early days, this usually was paid in kind. Some people paid the Church a tenth of their yearly profit in the form of cattle, leading to a large church herd. This herd, which grazed some ranges on the Arizona Strip under the management of Anson P. Winsor and family at Pipe Spring (now Pipe Spring National Monument), provided an additional resource for the Church, effectively supplementing the tithing income. Many builders and their families were nourished by the beef and dairy products from the Pipe Spring herd.

In 1863, St. George became the seat of Washington County. With the construction of the cotton factory in Washington giving promise of a market for this important crop, optimistic county officials met in 1866 and appropriated money for the basement of a courthouse. The

following year the electorate approved a tax of seven and a half mills to complete the building. It was finished in 1870 and provided (among other items) a three-cell jail in the basement, one cell of which had a steel door and no window. Here "very bad criminals were kept, such as cattle rustlers."

In 1871, Brigham Young further called upon the settlers in southern Utah to build a temple to serve Mormons throughout the area. Many factors no doubt figured in his decision: since he now wintered regularly in St. George, he could supervise construction of the building; the location would mean no seasonal interruptions; many of the necessary raw materials lay in the nearby hills; and perhaps more importantly, the men here needed work. No doubt the fact that some of them were skilled workers who had helped build temples in Ohio and Illinois also influenced his plans.

To finance the St. George temple, the Church drew on all tithing resources of southern Utah south of Fillmore, periodically sending great caravans of wagons to collect the people's offerings. Not only did these towns donate material goods but they also sent so many of their men to contribute labor that a bakery, a butcher shop, and boarding houses were constructed to care for them. The Church paid the workers in "T. O. Script," redeemable only at the above establishments and at the tithing office.

Brigham Young, who had built homes and spent many winters here, chose the site for the temple and arranged for its dedication. Excavation at his chosen spot had not proceeded far, however, before the men encountered sink holes and mud. Questioning the wisdom of building on such uncertain foundations, they asked their president to select another location, but he was adamant that the temple be built there. Obediently, therefore, the men built drains and went into the hills to procure lava for foundation stone.

Men had brought from California, probably from Sutter's Fort, a cannon, reputedly a remnant of Napoleon's invasion of Russia. It was found that, when filled with lead, the cannon made an excellent pile driver for hammering the heavy black stone into the earth, providing a solid foundation for the native red sandstone walls. Workers hauled the timbers from Mount Trumbull, 80 miles to the south. The $110,000 tabernacle was completed in 1876, and the following year the temple was dedicated, the first completed west of the Mississippi. This more elaborate structure cost about $800,000. Today, it is the oldest Mormon temple in the world still in use.

Although silk was produced as early as 1874, it did not add materially to the income of St. George. Nevertheless, the mulberry trees, which were planted to feed the worms, have provided welcome shade throughout all succeeding years. Visitors can today see fine examples outside Brigham Young's Winter Home on 200 North Street and the Grundy House on Main Street.

The mining boom at Silver Reef, just north of the city, was a significant economic aid for several years. It not only furnished employment for some of the inhabitants but also opened up a close and lucrative market for many of their crops. Despite the fact that Silver Reef, being populated by mostly non-Mormon miners represented a way of life that was anathema to the otherwise religious settlements of southern Utah, the boomtown's demise was an economic setback for the entire Washington County. The years of hardship and uncertainty ended in 1891, however, with the completion of the Washington Fields Dam, which brought the troublesome Rio Virgin under control.

In 1911, the Church established the St. George Stake Academy, later known as the Dixie Normal School, as a teacher training school. Eventually, the state took over the educational establishment and renamed it Dixie Junior College. The school now provides some four-year classes, two years of fully accredited college work for those who intend to secure a university degree, a computer center, and terminal, general, and vocational education for others.

The population of St. George has grown remarkably in the last decade, and the city's boundaries now touch Santa Clara on the west, Washington on the east, and the Arizona state line on the south. The agricultural base is now relatively small, but a new industrial community has emerged, which provides employment for many residents. Nowadays, though, tourism is becoming one of St. George's most important industries. St. George's proximity to Interstate 15, which brings travelers from southern California through the sizzling Mojave Desert to Utah, has led to increased visitation. St. George and Bluff boulevards are lined with a good selection of motels, restaurants, stores, and other visitor facilities.

St. George is consistently ranked in the top ten retirement communities in the nation. An increase in seasonal residents has led to a concomitant growth in the service industry, as well as greater involvement in cultural events, both of which have yielded benefits for the community. Despite its growth, St. George retains much of its small-town atmosphere, while emerging as an economic force in the state.

There is something for everyone in this clean, neatly laid out city, which boasts seven golf courses, many playing fields where large softball and soccer tournaments are held, tennis courts, an outdoor public swimming pool, several city parks,

Exploring the St. George Area

A number of short excursions can be made to the communities surrounding St. George.

Just north on Interstate 15 are Washington (site of the original Cotton Mill), Leeds, and Silver Reef, which now has a museum and art gallery in the old Wells Fargo building and is well worth a trip.

To the east is Zion National Park, which is bordered by a number of interesting historic communities and a ghost town. A day trip might take the visitor through the park, up Highway 89 through the agricultural Long Valley, turning west on Scenic Byway 14 and traveling through the alpine splendor of Cedar Breaks National Monument to Cedar City and back down to St. George.

West of St. George, another pleasant day's drive might take in Santa Clara, Ivins, Snow Canyon State Park, Gunlock Reservoir, Veyo (known for its hot springs), Central, a side trip to Pine Valley, and back to Highway 18 to the infamous Mountain Meadows, which figures so painfully in Mormon history. Turning right on Highway 56 at Enterprise takes the traveler past the iron-rich hills that give Iron County its name to Cedar City and back down Interstate 15 to St. George.

St. George is an excellent base for exploring southern Utah's Land of Color.

and nearby Quail Creek and Gunlock reservoirs for water sports and boating enthusiasts. Every year, St. George holds the Utah Seniors Golf Tournament, the World Senior Games, the Rotary Bowl, a 10-kilometer run, as well as the popular St. George Marathon, in addition to rodeos, the St. George Arts Festival, and many conventions.

Some excellent facilities and centers have been built, including shopping malls, an art museum, and the magnificent Dixie Center, which has added a further dimension to cultural events, recreation, athletics, and conventions. Plans are also afoot in the next couple of years to establish a bike route between Zion National Park and Gunlock Reservoir, with St. George as the central point.

Visitors are welcome to tour the classic Mormon tabernacle building, but non-Mormons may not enter the temple. The beautifully landscaped grounds around the temple are open to visitors, however, and a visitor center shows short films explaining the Mormon religion. Brigham Young's Winter Home is a popular destination for many visitors. The Daughters of the Utah Pioneers Museum, located behind the old county courthouse on St. George Boulevard (now the Chamber of Commerce building), also houses many wonderful exhibits, including items from Brigham Young's bedroom and other pioneer artifacts.

SANTA CLARA

Elevation: 2,750 feet; population: 2,322.

Spanish-speaking travelers, who came through here on the Old Spanish Trail (later the Mormon Trail) during the 1830s and 1840s, first applied the name Santa Clara to the stream that waters this town. *Santa* is a Spanish word for "female saint" and *Clara* means "a short interval of fair weather." The native Paiutes called the creek *tonaquaint*, "a stream carrying black silt."

The first Anglo settlement on the Santa Clara was made in December 1854 by eight men from New Harmony sent here as missionaries to the Paiute Indians, who grew corn and other crops along the Santa Clara Creek. The missionaries had first visited the Paiutes here in June and in the intervening months one of their number, Jacob Hamblin, had spent considerable time working with them, with the result that a friendly relationship now existed between the native people and the new arrivals.

The missionaries spent the winter of 1854–1855 building a dam in the stream, breaking ground, and digging irrigation ditches with the help of the Paiutes. When Hamblin became ill from exposure, one of the settlers, Augustus P. Hardy, rode north to Harmony for medicine, which was quickly dispatched to the ailing Hamblin. Continuing to Parowan, Hardy was given a quart of cotton seed by Sister Nancy Anderson, a pioneer woman who had come from the South. The men planted the cotton a seed at a time and husbanded it with meticulous care throughout the growing season.

With the promise of an abundant harvest, early that fall some of the missionaries moved their families to the "Tonaquint Station." The families gathered the cotton crop, picked the seeds out by hand, spun the fibers on a spinning wheel, and the women wove 30 yards of cloth on a "loom of the most primitive make." A sample of the cloth sent to Brigham Young, who had it carefully analyzed and tested, eventually resulted in the organization of the Cotton Mission, which established so many communities in Utah's Dixie.

Acting on the counsel of church leaders, the Santa Clara inhabitants spent the winter of 1856–1857 constructing a protective 100-square-yard rock fort. The following summer they harvested excellent crops, and before the year's end, additional settlers arrived to strengthen the colony. In 1858 the threat of war between the Mormons and the United States government, occasioned by the march of Johnston's army toward the Utah Territory, prompted the recall to Utah of Mormon settlers in San Bernardino, California. Some of this group settled at Santa Clara. Several varieties of fruit trees, which had been planted earlier, were now producing sizeable crops, and the Church had great hopes for Santa Clara.

In May 1861, President Brigham Young visited the settlement. Although he complimented the people on their progress, he was concerned about their location and advised them to move their homes farther back from the creek in order to escape the danger of floods. In common with other settlements in southern Utah, the pioneers of Santa Clara battled constantly with the usually meager flow of Santa Clara Creek. In summer, water shortages caused arguments between the Indians and the settlers as to who should be allowed irrigation water. But in winter, heavy rains threatened the safety of the whole settlement as angry floodwaters broke through dams and flooded the banks of the river, destroying everything in their path.

No doubt Brigham Young's impression of the area was generally favorable, however, for, in October 1861, at the General Church Conference, he and other leaders organized the "Dixie Mission." Included in those "called" were about 30 families of Swiss immigrants. Many of this group were poor and, lacking transportation facilities, had to depend upon the Perpetual Emigration Fund of the Church and on their fellow Mormons for assistance in getting to their new homes. Arriving here on November 28, 1861, they found arrangements had been made for them to take up land at the present town site. In December, authorities made a survey and provided property for everyone who needed it; however, that was the fateful month the Great Rain began.

The Great Rain was especially destructive in Santa Clara. By January the continual downpour, which had thoroughly saturated the ground, culminated in a huge flood. Not only did it wash out acres of valuable farmland and orchards, but also undermined and destroyed part of the rock fort and carried a molasses mill, grist mill, and a homemade cotton gin into the Rio Virgin. The problem of starting anew faced the old settlers and the Swiss alike.

The story of the battle for survival that the Swiss colony experienced is rich in drama and the details of human achievement. For the most part those stalwart people could not speak English, they did not know the country, and they were poor. Faced with the lack of farming equipment they relied heavily on sweat, courage, and faith. The final straw was the malaria, caused by proximity to the river, which plagued the weakened population.

With their fields and orchards destroyed by the flood, many of the older settlers left the impoverished village. But the persistent, frugal Swiss remained. Despite their many problems they slowly but steadily stabilized their economy until, by 1873, their donations to the Church to care for the poor were sent elsewhere, "they having no poor in Santa Clara." Drainage of the swamps in 1880 relieved the malaria problem.

Export of fruit and garden crops has long been a source of income for Santa Clara people. For many years they have carried their produce to nearby towns, first in wagons, and later in trucks. Many Utah and Nevada communities, not blessed with the long growing season that this area enjoys, have for years looked forward to the arrival of the "Dixie Peddler" in the early summer. Santa Clara residents have developed the industry so thoroughly that a fleet of trucks not only markets the produce of the town but also procures fruit and vegetables from California and Arizona to provide a year-round supply for neighboring communities. Streetside stands selling fruit are a common sight here in summer.

Visitors to Santa Clara will enjoy visiting the attractive home of Mormon missionary Jacob Hamblin, which was renovated by the state in the 1960s. The Mormon Church now operates tours of the home, which lies at the far end of the village. In addition, a new arboretum in the Santa Clara Heights, consisting of a scenic trail cut through a sharp, black lava flow, is a delightful side trip. The population of Santa Clara has grown markedly in recent years, as a result of its proximity to St. George. It is easily reached, just four miles northwest of St. George on Highway 91.

Jacob Hamblin

Jacob Hamblin was one of a handful of missionaries "called" to work with the native people of southern Utah and beyond. His sensitivity to Indian affairs enabled him to act as a trusted mediator between the native people and his own people, resulting in 1857 in his appointment as president of the Southern Indian Mission.

Hamblin spent most of his life working among the Indian tribes of the Southwest, bringing many of them into the Mormon faith, teaching them European ways, and interceding in the many disputes arising from misunderstandings and competition for limited resources between American Indians and white settlers.

Life on the frontier was complicated by ever-changing alliances between Indian and Indian, and Indian and white; those whites interested in settling on the traditional lands of the Utes, Paiutes, Navajos, and Hopis were glad of Hamblin's help. Despite being a skilled diplomat, even Hamblin occasionally encountered difficulties in resolving grievances. In 1874, he almost lost his life to the Navajos, who were blaming the Mormons for killing two of their men and demanding expensive compensation for their loss. Hamblin stood his ground, denying any wrongdoing by his people, and eventually gained the respect of the Navajo leaders.

In the early 1870s, Hamblin became a valuable guide for famed explorer Major John Wesley Powell in his travels among the many Indian tribes of the Southwest. In 1870, he and Hamblin worked together to achieve an important peace treaty with the Navajo. The Mormon missionary's assistance enabled Powell and his colleagues to move among the tribes, studying the native cultures. Powell went on to report some of the Indians' concerns back in Washington, D.C.

Jacob Hamblin home, Santa Clara

SHUNESBURG

Elevation: 4,000; population: 0.

Following the Great Rain, which carried away considerable quantities of arable land along the Virgin, five families from Rockville, who had lost acreage, moved upriver and established Shunesburg. Arriving January 20, 1862, they

Silver-bearing sandstones lie on both sides of the Virgin Anticline east and west of the little village of Leeds. Of the several explanations offered concerning the origin of this exceedingly rare deposit, one of the most interesting ones suggests that the silver originally came from the volcanic tuffs that make up the Chinle Formation of the Triassic Era. These beds are known to contain small quantities of silver and other minerals. Over these beds, in the Silver Reef area, ancient streams deposited the Silver Reef Sandstone (Springdale member of the Moenave Formation). This rock contains fossil wood—usually in the form of fragments of petrified trees, bushes, reeds, and logs. Subsequent to the deposition of the sand and the wood, water dissolved the silver and carried it upward in solution. As the silver-bearing water neared the decaying vegetation, chemical changes resulting from the decay caused the water to precipitate out and become deposited in both the sand and petrified material. The nearer the Silver Reef miners came to the petrified wood, the richer became the sandstone.

Following the upfolding of the Virgin Anticline, the Silver Reef area has been faulted at least twice. The rich "White Reef" is thought to be an overthrust that developed during one of these periods of faulting. The nearby "Buckeye Reef" is part of a small upfold known as the Leeds Anticline and represents the same original sedimentary layer.

purchased land from the Paiute Indian Chief Shunes (for whom the town was named) and immediately began building log cabins and preparing the land for planting.

From the start, the river proved intransigent; and not until 1865 were the settlers able to harvest good crops of cotton, corn, and cane. By that time, nevertheless, a dozen families were living at Shunesburg. In 1866, fruit trees that had been planted earlier were producing a good crop. That same year also saw the construction of the "Wiggle Trail," which led up the precipitous cliffs and crags to the plateau, connecting Shunesburg with Kanab and the Long Valley communities. (Early scientific maps and papers refer to this as the Wriggle Trail, but local people, who built the trail and named it, claim that they wiggle, not wriggle.) The trail served as a route by which the townsfolk took livestock to their ranges atop the mesa. Later that year, the families moved to Rockville for safety during the period of Indian unrest caused by the Blackhawk War.

In 1868, a few of the original settlers were joined by several families of newcomers in the re-settling of Shunesburg. Sometime during the next two years, civil authorities inaugurated mail service between Kanab and Toquerville, with riders delivering the mail twice weekly. So as to avoid the steep and tortuous Wiggle Trail, riders from both ends of the route carried their mail pouches to Shunesburg, or to the plateau above, where they raised or lowered them over a long wire windlass. (David Flanigan was later to use this idea as a basis for building his own cable in Zion Canyon.)

Major John Wesley Powell made this village his temporary headquarters in 1872. Two years later, Brigham Young visited the outpost and organized the United Order, which lasted two years here, then failed.

An outstanding landmark at Shunesburg is Oliver De Mille's 20-by-56-foot cut stone residence. Built between 1882 and 1889 on the site of some Indian ruins, this large, two-storied house served also as a recreational center for this and nearby towns for several years.

In the meantime, floods in the Virgin continued to take their toll. With the great increase in livestock on the range destroying much of the essential plant cover that held the soil, each year was marked by a decrease in available acreage. Year by year, the people left the little hamlet until, by 1900, only De Mille and his family remained. In 1902, he also deserted the desolate outpost. At Shunesburg, the victor was the Rio Virgin.

Located about 2.5 miles up Parunuweap Canyon, the ghost town of Shunesburg is no longer accessible to visitors. The town is located on private property, and the landowner will not give permission for people to drive or walk across his property. The only exceptions are hikers hiking downstream through Parunuweap Canyon who have advance permission from the landowner.

SILVER REEF

Elevation: 4,000 feet; population: incorporated into town of Leeds

The scanty remains of the once bustling mining community of Silver Reef lie two miles north of Leeds, of which it is now a part. The ghost town is reached via a paved road that leaves the highway in the northeast end of that quiet town. In recent years, Silver Reef has become a popular destination for visitors to the St. George area, and a large subdivision is growing up in the immediate vicinity.

The stone Wells Fargo building was restored in 1986 and now houses the Silver Reef Museum, displaying many fascinating historic artifacts, as well as an art gallery highlighting the bronze sculptures of acclaimed local sculptor Jerry Anderson. The old powder house in the back of the building contains a scale model of Silver Reef during its heyday in the 1880s. Detailed, handmade models of some of the key buildings are also exhibited in adjacent display cases. Renovation of the bank building across the street began in 1991. The tailings from the old mines may still be seen, together with some of the early mining equipment. The elevated location and 360-degree views make this an excellent location to view the striking southern Utah sunsets.

Silver was first discovered here about 1866 when John Kemple, a prospector, found silver float in Quail Creek. Although Kemple moved to Nevada for a number of years, he returned in 1874 and was instrumental in the formulation and adoption of a code of laws and constitution for the Harrisburg Mining District.

Several stories are told about the discovery of the mother lode. One tale depicts silver oozing from a hot fireplace in a Leeds residence built from the sandstone. Others maintain that the following grindstone story reached Salt Lake City and induced prospectors to come to the area: Residents from Leeds were in the habit of quarrying sandstone from the white "reefs" west of town. From this they shaped grindstones, some of which were exported for sale in Pioche, Nevada. In Pioche lived an assayer whom the miners had dubbed "Metaliferous" Murphy because of his reputed ability to find ore in dubious samples of rock. One of the grindstones from Leeds had been broken, and a group decided to test Murphy's reputation by preparing a sample from the broken stone. Although silver had been found in sandstone in a German mine hundreds of years before, few people knew of it, and prospectors generally considered such an occurrence quite impossible (Silver Reef is still the only place in the United States where this has occurred). Consequently, the men of Pioche considered Murphy's affirmative report of rich silver chloride in the rock sufficient evidence of his unreliability. Some records say that the miners then expelled him from camp. The story, in general, seems to have a factual basis, but there is no record of the date of this event, and some

folks maintain that it took place after the prospectors located the mother lode.

The most reasonable account appears to be one citing two Leeds residents who, following the organization of the Harrisburg Mining District and the flurry of prospecting that attended it, located a claim and sent samples to Walker Brothers in Salt Lake City for analysis. The positive results of the tests prompted Walker Brothers to send William Tecumseh Barbee and others to the district to make observations. They arrived at the mining camp on Quail Creek in June 1875 and, by October, had procured an assaying outfit. The following month, as two residents from Harrisburg hauled a wagon load of wood over the Buckeye Reef, the wheels of their vehicle tore loose some rock. When Barbee passed the fresh exposure, quite by accident, his trained eye detected the precious metal.

Apparently for almost a year the information regarding the find was not well known, for only about a dozen miners worked in the area. At first they shipped the ore to Salt Lake City, but since lower freight rates and milling costs could be secured by sending it to Pioche, they hauled most of it there. In November miners from Pioche began to migrate to southern Utah, starting what was known as the "Pioche Stampede."

Barbee had picked a site for his "Bonanza City" on a flat east of the rich Tecumseh Claim on the Buckeye Reef; however, when Hyrum Jacobs, a Pioche merchant, visited the camp, he also saw a rich opportunity to do business here. Choosing a site north of Barbee's location, he loaded the stock of his Pioche store in wagons, took his building down in sections, and hauled it to the chosen spot. He named the place Silver Reef, after the white, silver-bearing rocky "reefs" near his store. To serve the flood of prospectors, a

saloon was soon built nearby, and a restaurant offered "hash at all hours." Eventually, as Silver Reef and Bonanza City grew toward each other, the name Silver Reef won out.

The wisdom of extracting the silver locally soon became evident. In 1877, therefore, companies built two mills: the five-stamp Leeds Mill and the three-stamp Pioneer Mill. Both mills refined the ore by the pan-amalgamation process. Also that year, a newspaper called the *Silver Reef Echo* began publication.

During the next two years, with two more stamp mills constructed, the town grew rapidly. Homes, schools, a bank, laundries, bakeries, butcher shops, saloons, a gambling house, a Chinatown (housing Chinese railroad workers who had migrated to the town in search of work), and all the essentials of a mining town were steadily added. Much to the chagrin of the surrounding Mormon communities, a brothel also began operation. The Wells Fargo Express hauled the bullion to the railroad terminals. Although smaller outfits also operated, four main companies gained control of most of the production.

Silver Reef reached its peak during the late 1870s and early 1880s, when silver sold for $1.17 an ounce. Where the sandstone contained fossil plants, it was especially rich. Often there was silver in the petrified wood found in the Moenave Formation; one such log yielded 17,000 ounces of silver. Even though there is no exact record of the number of people living here (the population fluctuated between a handful of people and just under 2,000), there were enough residents for Silver Reef seriously to contemplate trying to secure the Washington County seat. This would have required enough registered voters to outnumber voters in all other Washington County towns.

By 1881 the price of silver was declining,

Snow Canyon State Park

and the mine operators were encountering problems with ground water in many of their shafts. An attempt to solve these probems by cutting wages from $4 to $3.50 a day resulted in a paralyzing strike. Although, at length, the matter was settled, the steady decline in the price of silver made operations increasingly difficult.

The possibility of obtaining the county seat vanished on March 9, 1882, when the territorial legislature, prompted by local Mormon leaders (who were aghast at the idea of Silver Reef becoming the county seat), passed an act that moved the county line some 20 miles eastward, thereby bringing a half dozen more towns into the county. Significantly, the act stipulated that it should "take effect for election purposes on and after the first day, of July, 1882."

By 1891 all Silver Reef companies had ceased operation, and miners were working on a lease basis. Two years later, Wooley, Lund, and Judd, a mercantile establishment at the Reef, secured winter water rights on Quail Creek and converted the Barbee-Walker Mill to water power. As a consequence, miners were again able to make good wages, and the company prospered. In 1896, a Cleveland company purchased the

holdings of Wooley, Lund, and Judd, but further decline in the price of silver made their operation impracticable.

Near the turn of the century many Silver Reef buildings were offered for sale to the highest bidder. Peter Anderson of Anderson's Ranch purchased the old dance hall. Its original owner had been shot and during the following night had died of his wound. While dismantling the building, Anderson found $2,000 in gold coins. Others immediately followed Anderson's lead, purchasing many of the old buildings and promptly tearing them down; but no one else was as lucky as he.

Mining at Silver Reef became sporadic from then on. In 1916, Alex Colbath began acquiring mining rights at Silver Reef. Subsequently, parts of the holdings were secured by the American Smelting and Refining Company, which sank a shaft, pumped out the groundwater on the lower slopes, and began to extract the ore. This operation ended much like previous ventures at the Reef, with a decline in the price of silver that made operation of the mine unprofitable. In 1952 Western Gold and Uranium acquired the properties, extracting silver and uranium ore until 1959, when again, an unfavorable market closed the operation. The mill was reopened for a time in 1961 and processed copper ore from the Apex Mine west of St. George.

Although mining operations have now ceased, Silver Reef's early history profoundly affected southern Utah. Indeed, Silver Reef brought this remote area of Utah to the attention of the outside world, bringing many changes to the isolated existence of the original Dixie pioneers. Existing records give an accounting of more than $10.5 million worth of silver shipped from Silver Reef; however, some people point out that part of the profit was never recorded, and that as

much as $17 million may actually have been made. Nevertheless, during the hardest years of Mormon settlement in this rugged country, the boomtown gave the people of the surrounding communities, who were struggling to build their settlements and survive floods, droughts, illness, and disillusionment, a ready market for their produce, wines, and handmade items. And the boom town was responsible for moving a county line.

SNOW CANYON STATE PARK

Elevation: 3,400 feet.

One of the most popular recreational areas for St. George residents and visitors alike is Snow Canyon State Park, which is reached via a 24-mile loop west from St. George. The dramatic desert scenery on view here combines red Navajo Sandstone and lava formations in a unique setting. Camping, picnicking, and horseback riding facilities are available; and a number of backcountry hikes offer an excellent opportunity to observe specially adapted desert plants and animals, as well as the complicated, turbulent geological forces that have shaped this canyon. Hence, the surreal desert landscape of Snow Canyon has been a favorite location for film makers over the years.

During some presently undetermined interval, the Snow Canyon area was subjected to crustal forces that uplifted it, tilted it northward, and shattered its resistant rocks to produce an almost perfectly straight fracture zone with a strike 10 degrees west of north, and a second running 27 degrees east of north.

During the volcanic activity that built Pine Valley Mountain, possibly during Miocene times, a host of radial streams developed on the mountain's flanks. One of these, Rock Hollow Wash, ran in a southwesterly direction through what is now Dammeron Valley. Erosion caused these radial streams and their tributaries to strip the grey Cretaceous sandstones and shales from the mountain's flanks, at the same time as the Vermilion Cliffs were eroding northward from the Virgin River Basin.

With the protective cover stripped from its surface, the shattered Snow Canyon fracture zone became more vulnerable to stream erosion. Broken rocks were easily removed, resulting in several parallel drainages that eroded northward, following the fracture planes. During this period, black basaltic lava flowed in low places down Pine Valley Mountain from a source presently unknown. Part of this flow may be seen rising above St. George Airport, where it forms thin outliers to the north.

Eventually, the easternmost of the straight drainages in the Snow Canyon fracture zone captured the waters of Rock Hollow Wash just below Dammeron Valley and carried them southward to the Virgin River near the wash's present confluence with the Santa Clara Creek. The action of these waters carved an ancestral Snow Canyon, which was then covered by lava flows that burst forth a second time from at least two sources. The flows filled the canyon floor from the northern entrance to the present park as far as the Virgin River.

With its channel effectively blocked by the lava, the waters from Rock Hollow Wash now began to run westward, encountering a second straight-walled drainage channel, which diverted them southward, thereby setting in motion the excavation of the present Snow Canyon. At about the same time, a separate lava flow ran down Wide Canyon, directing its waters southward into Dammeron Valley to supplement those from Rock Hollow Wash.

The last volcanic eruptions here occurred in Dammeron Valley, where lava flows not only filled part of the valley and created an effective barrier at its southern end but also ran down through Snow Canyon to the Santa Clara Creek. Behind the lava dam the valley has been filled with streamborne silt. Cinder cones grew up atop the flows in Dammeron Valley which, even today, have a remarkably fresh appearance, despite their age. Both lava flows contain lava tubes, caused by subterranean molten lava flowing through faster-cooling surface lava. Some of these lava tubes may be entered and explored (Anasazi Indians once used them for shelter); other tubes are less visible, located only by the movement of air of varying intensity in and out of the cracks in their roofs as the atmospheric pressure changes.

SPRINGDALE

Elevation: 3,900 feet; population: 275.

Springdale, 45 miles northwest of St. George, is next to Zion National Park's South Entrance. Visitors will find this attractive town, with its choice of accommodations, restaurants, and services, an excellent base from which to explore the park and the area beyond.

The original community of Springdale, first settled in the autumn of 1862, was located just south of the present town. The name was chosen because of the nearby springs, which, incidentally, made much of the nearby land swampy, providing excellent breeding grounds for mosquitoes carrying malaria—a severe problem for early settlers.

During the first winter, there was such a rapid increase in the population of this outpost that by winter's end 20 families were sheltered here in dugouts, log cabins, and willow houses. Despite flooding, Springdale pioneers were less affected by heavy rains than were some other Virgin River Valley residents, and were able to persevere with cultivating their farmlands.

Nevertheless, life was sufficiently hard that, by 1864, over half the families had moved away. Then, in 1866, fears of Indian unrest sparked by the Blackhawk War prompted the balance of the settlers to move to Rockville for a time, although several men continued to cultivate their Springdale fields, traveling far every day to carry out the work. Some of the settlers moved back to their homes in 1869, followed the next year by others, but several families never returned. Continued problems with malaria forced the residents to migrate from the swampy lowlands to the present town site. Eventually, the swamp was drained and the accursed disease finally brought under control.

Springdale's isolation made life difficult. Removed, as they were, from the principal routes of travel, the inhabitants were forced to supply themselves with many of the necessities of life. One of their homemade items, the rawhide-bottomed chair, proved so sturdy and desirable that in time it was exported. For a time, not long ago, the manufacture of this chair, as well as other pioneer furniture and ornaments, was revived in Springdale; however, this activity has since disappeared, to be replaced in popularity by rock shops.

Though the residents' farms ran well into Zion Canyon, the amount of arable land was limited, and access to grazing lands in the top country was difficult. The townspeople arrived at a partial solution to this latter problem by constructing the Big Bend Trail to the East Rim (the East Rim Trail in Zion National Park now follows the approximate route of the earlier trail).

Springdale has been strongly affected by the steady development of Zion National Park, which was first protected as Mukuntuweap National

Monument (1909), and then Zion National Park (1919). A local resident, Walter Ruesch, became the first custodian of the national monument and figured importantly in developing many roads and trails. Over the years, construction of recreational facilities by the government, as well as development of accommodations by concessionaires, has provided a number of residents with work in the adjoining park. However, increased park visitation has also forced this little town to consider how much development of visitor services it wishes to accommodate without losing its identity. It is unlikely that the original settlers of this once-remote outpost could ever have imagined the challenges now facing the leaders of Springdale; yet, the Dixie pioneer spirit, which still permeates the community today, makes it likely that this historic community will find its own answers to the complex issues ahead.

SUMMIT

Elevation: 6,150 feet; population: 101 (unofficial) NO FIGS.

Summit, which derives its name from its elevated position on the alluvial fan built up by Summit Creek over a period of many years, follows Brian Head in having the highest elevation of any town in Iron County. Because the Walker Indian War threatened their safety, the single family that settled here first in 1853 did not stay long. The site remained deserted until 1856, when two settlers from Enoch moved here, followed shortly by two more families. Feeling the need for more people, the inhabitants wrote Brigham Young requesting the addition of a small group, stating that they would provide 160 acres of land, as well as the waters of the creek for irrigation each Friday. This section of the Summit field is still spoken of as the "Friday" section, and one sixth of

the water supply is bought and sold as a "Friday."

Brigham Young responded to the colonizers' request for assistance by "calling" six more men to Summit. In 1859, the people surveyed the town and began construction of homes on their lots. As the Blackhawk War loomed in 1866, the townspeople constructed a protective adobe fort enclosing about an acre of land, which they used until the native unrest diminished.

Many of the current residents still make their living by farming, although some now commute to nearby Cedar City to work. Summit is located halfway between Cedar City and Parowan on the old U.S. Highway 91, now bypassed by Interstate 15. Tourist facilities may be found at the interchange in the form of a truck stop.

TOQUERVILLE

Elevation: 3,400 feet; population: 488.

The big spring of clear, pure water of central importance to generations of Paiute Indians was first reported by whites in 1852, when John D. Lee and other pioneers from the Iron Mission explored the area with a view to settling farther south. Five years later, a favorable report on the site by Isaac C. Haight and other residents from Cedar City led to six families from Cedar City and Harmony moving here in February 1858. A few Mormon families from San Bernardino, California, soon joined them, following their recall to Utah by the Church.

The Paiutes then living at the springs were led by a chief named Toquer, who was highly respected in the area and who seems to have agreed to allow the Mormon pioneers to settle at the springs. The chief had apparently received his name as a result of his dark complexion, the word *toquer* being the Paiute word for "black." Opinion

is mixed, though, as to whether the new Mormon colony was named for the chief or for the black basalt rocks of the Hurricane Bench that are a distinctive feature of the town.

When a heavy hail storm ruined much of the cotton and other crops during their first year of occupation, the colonizers of Toquerville became very discouraged. Nevertheless, the Church counseled the group to remain and persevere, with the result that, by 1859, 19 families resided here. Since one early settler was a brickmaker by trade, homes constructed of burned brick soon appeared, which may still be seen.

During the first two years, the principal crops to be planted in this new Dixie settlement were typical of those recommended by the Church: cotton, corn, sorghum cane, and garden vegetables. One man built a hand-operated cotton gin, the first in southern Utah, while another used the waters of Ash Creek to power a flour mill. Molasses from their Chinese sorghum cane found a ready market in northern settlements, where it was used for canning fruit.

The Great Rain of 1861–1862 affected most of the fledgling Dixie communities adversely. At Toquerville, however, it caused Ash Creek to cut a deeper channel and to open up new springs. Some of the people "called" to the Cotton Mission that winter located at Toquerville, bringing seeds and cuttings with them that led to the lush vineyards and heavily laden orchards for which Toquerville became famous.

Since all fruit grew well, the settlers soon had a surplus. In 1866, Washington County officials granted Toquerville a license to distill wine. The next season they issued two more permits. Here, it appeared, was a product that was not perishable, and one that could be sold to outsiders for cash. Brigham Young advised the

Tropic Ditch

residents to dispose of their grapes in the following manner: "First by lightly pressing, make a light wine. Then give a heavier pressing and make colored wine. Then barrel up this wine and if my counsel is taken, this wine will not be drunk here but will be exported..."

The finest wine, called Nail's Best, was produced by John C. Naile (usually known as Naegle) who constructed a two-story winery from native sandstone. Unfortunately, the people did not heed Brigham Young's advice regarding home consumption, nor did they exercise sufficient care in the selection of good wine for export. Consequently, the market for the product did not hold up, and the local drinking habit became common enough to cause concern. Church leaders finally discouraged the manufacture of the intoxicant altogether. The big rock building, with its spacious wine cellar, which gave so much promise of a lucrative income, still stands adjacent to the highway in the south end of the village. It has since been restored and converted into a private residence. A plaque now marks the building as an historic site.

In 1869 "Tokerville" became the county seat of Kane County and, until 1883, cared for civil affairs of this pioneer political unit. The Mormon Church's experiment with the United Order, a strictly cooperative venture instituted by Brigham Young in 1874, lasted only a few months here, as it did in most areas of Dixie. Even though

the boom at Silver Reef provided a good market for the farmers' produce in the late 1870s and early 1880s, that town was the major factor in causing Toquerville to lose the county seat and be transfered back to Washington County.

Fruit and field crops continue to be important to Toquerville's economy. Livestock grazed on the nearby plateaus supplement this income. Despite its proximity to Interstate 15, just north of St. George, the pretty little village of Toquerville still seems delightfully untouched by the outside world.

TROPIC

Elevation: 6,300 feet; population: 380.

Before the turn of the century, the pioneers of the Paria Valley became aware of the problems of erosion and the lack of life-giving water. Although there was good arable land in the upper valley, experience had shown that the streams there were neither large nor dependable enough for irrigation. The situation was further aggravated by the presence atop the nearby Paunsagunt Plateau of a copious stream, the East Fork of the Sevier River. Even though an early attempt to divert this water into the basin had not been successful, the people had not forgotten its possibilities. In 1888, therefore, the residents proposed digging a ditch to secure this water. A stock company was formed to carry out the project, and the elected leaders immediately laid plans to survey and build the necessary ditch. The expectation of water prompted some people to move into the Upper Paria or Bryce Valley in the winter of 1890–1891, where they surveyed a town site the following year.

Though the work on the ditch was arduous, and at times discouraging, in May 1892 water was successfully brought "over the rim of the basin,"

marking the only place where a sizeable stream has been diverted from the Great Basin into another drainage area. After a joyous celebration, the people held a meeting to decide on the name for the new community. Surprisingly, they chose to call their community Tropic, apparently because they felt that the climate here contrasts so markedly with that of the plateau above.

Tropic's moderate climate allows fruit to grow well, and agriculture and ranching are still the mainstays of the economy here. Coal is mined in the nearby hills for local consumption and some export. A few residents commute to work at Bryce Canyon. One of Tropic's pioneers was Ebenezer Bryce, for whom Bryce Canyon was named. His original log cabin may still be seen in Tropic. A few visitor services are available here.

VEYO

Elevation: 4,500 feet; population: 500.

The town of Veyo, which is 19 miles northwest of St. George, rests on a lava flow that once impounded the Santa Clara Creek. Before the stream could cut its way through the igneous rock, a veneer of streamborne alluvium was deposited in a lake. Today, Veyo is perhaps best known for Veyo Resort, which offers a swimming pool fed by odor-free mineral hot springs that occur as a direct consequence of the area's volcanic past.

For a number of years, before he obtained a survey to back his hunch, James L. Bunker was convinced that the water from the Santa Clara Creek could be brought out onto the level land at Veyo. A favorable survey, made in 1911, led Bunker to apply for high water rights in the creek. Beginning the next winter, Bunker and interested friends from nearby farms took advantage of the off-season lull in agricultural pursuits to build the necessary irrigation ditch. Almost all the labor was paid for by the sale of stock in the irrigation company.

The water began irrigating the fields in the spring of 1914. Plagued from the beginning by operational problems with their ditch, within two years the colonizers had worked out a cooperative agreement with a power company to enlarge and strengthen it, allowing part of the water to be used to generate hydroelectric power. This agreement not only reduced the community's irrigation problems but the jobs created by the construction of the power plant helped the local economy.

The settlers were anxious to set up a school, with the result that a schoolhouse began operating in a canvas-covered frame building during the 1916–1917 school year. By Thanksgiving of the following year, the pupils were able to move into a purpose-built schoolhouse. That year, also, saw the establishing of a post office. When postal authorities rejected the name Glen Cove as being too common, the name Veyo was coined, a contraction of the words verdure and youth.

The residents of Veyo continue to depend largely upon farming and livestock raising for most of their livelihood. Veyo Resort, built in 1927, provides an additional income for the community.

Chocolate Cliffs

The best display of the variegated sandstones, limestones, gypsums, and shales that constitute the Chocolate Cliffs of the Moenkopi Formation is located in the vicinity of Virgin City. These rocks rest on the same heavy Kaibab limestone that forms the rim of the Grand Canyon. The chocolate-red Moenkopi Formation was once mud deposited along the margins of a shallow sea at the beginning of the Triassic period 240 to 245 million years ago. The resisistant, grey Shinarump (from the Paiute word *shinar*, meaning "wolf," and rump) conglomerate, a member of the Chinle Formation, is a stream deposit that was laid down atop the Moenkopi Formation. Here, it protects the softer shales beneath it and forms the caprock to the mesas. Petrified wood from ancient forests is common in the Chinle Formation and may be seen here. Highway 9 steadily climbs through these ancient strata and surmounts them two miles east of Rockville, at a point where the road turns north, affording the first view of Zion Canyon.

The near-level crest of the Hurricane Mesa, between the highway and the town of Virgin, has a space-age history. Between 1954 and 1962, under contract with the U.S. Air Force, the Coleman Engineering Company constructed and began operation of a test track that was firmly anchored into the mesa's solid caprock. During these tests (which continue today) rocket-propelled sleds speed down the track at supersonic speeds to discharge an intricately wired dummy airman—known as Hurricane Sam—over the precipitous southern ledge. The experiments test the effectiveness of various escape devices from aircraft traveling at high speeds.

VIRGIN CITY

Elevation: 3,400 feet; population: 229.

The first white man to explore the lands along the Rio Virgin above the Hurricane Fault was probably Mormon missionary Nephi Johnson. Johnson was sent into the area in the fall of 1858 to scout out new locations for communities. Recognized as one of the best interpreters of the Paiute Indian language in the territory, Johnson fraternized easily with the band of Paiutes living near Toquerville. He persuaded them to guide him over the rugged escarpment known as the Hurricane Cliffs, and up the river as far as the narrows of Zion Canyon.

Johnson found several sites suitable for settlement. Since no road existed at that early date, he was asked to return in December with a group of men and prepare a wagon road. The resulting tortuous roadway, known as the Johnson Twist, enabled the men to get their vehicles onto the plateau before the end of the month. Settlers at once made preparations to farm. The sod-lined banks of the Rio Virgin were easily dammed, allowing easy irrigation for new farmlands.

In April, using homemade instruments, the people laid out a town site. Originally known as Pocketville, after the Paiute word *pockich* meaning "cove," the residents soon changed the name to Virgin City in honor of the river. Although the village did not then have a city charter, the adoption of this name enabled the people to differentiate between the town and the river (and, by using "city" seems to indicate an optimistic attitude toward the town's future).

During the first two years the people were able to raise good crops, but the village's location on the floodplain of the Rio Virgin—considered such a boon at first—soon proved problematic. Unbeknownst to the settlers, the turbulent Rio Virgin had a history of flooding its banks during particularly heavy rainstorms. One such flood occurred during the summer of 1861, destroying the dam, which then had to be repaired—necessitating much extra labor and expense and reducing their harvest. The arrival of new settlers that autumn as part of the Cotton Mission, provided much needed encouragement.

The Great Rain of 1861 seriously affected the pioneers of Virgin City and neigboring communities on the Virgin River. The flood carried away much of their bottomlands, washed out or filled their ditches, and made the badly dissected stream channel much more difficult to dam. Subsequent troubles led some residents to request permission to move closer to their fields. As a result, a few residents built a small outpost (known as Dalton) a couple of miles upstream. Dalton was abandoned in 1866 as a result of the Blackhawk War, which threatened its safety. Augmented by the influx of people from nearby towns, who had been advised to band together to protect themselves from Indian unrest, Virgin City reached a population of more than 500 souls.

Oil was discovered near Virgin in 1907 as a result of a serendipitous meeting. Apparently, an elderly gentleman in distressed circumstances stopped at a mine near Tonopah, Nevada, to water his horses. Since water was scarce, and he and his animals both needed rest, he spent several days in the neighborhood. His troubles, he told the miners, were due to a fire that had occurred in southern Utah. He had built a cabin there, which he had hoped to heat by constructing a fireplace. The fireplace, fashioned from dark-colored rock, did just the opposite: the first time a fire was lit in it the rock became a mass of flame, causing the cabin to burn down. The Tonopah miners, almost certain that the rock contained oil, questioned the old man further about the location of the cabin and found out that it was situated near Duncan's Retreat in Washington County, Utah. They organized a company and sent some men to Virgin City to investigate.

Finding that there indeed was oil, the miners explored the area thoroughly and sank 15 shafts in an attempt to tap the liquid. Although some wells produced as much as 15 barrels of crude oil a day, most were dry, and the lack of a ready market, coupled with the financial handicaps caused by a depression that year, brought operations to an early halt.

Oil exploration was revived in the district in 1918, when operators cleared three producing wells, brought in a fourth, and built a refinery on North Creek large enough to handle 800 gallons of crude per shift. Despite the fact that, by 1920,

the four wells were producing about 20 barrels of crude oil a day, the operation proved economically unfeasible and petered out.

Livestock, agriculture, and fruit production are the principal occupations in Virgin. A partially paved Scenic Byway, leading to the Kolob Terrace and on to Cedar City (when not blocked by winter snow), joins Highway 9 within the town—look for the sign. The road climbs past ranches, through lovely countryside amid splendid red Navajo Sandstone formations. It provides the only easy access to the back of Zion National Park, which is 15 miles to the east. Several long hikes linking the two park units traverse this area. The road passes in and out of the national park on its way up to Kolob Reservoir, a popular place for trout fishing and camping (although there are no developed facilities).

WASHINGTON

Elevation: 2,750 feet; population: 4,198.

The town of Washington lies immediately northeast of St. George, just south of a break in the earth's crust known as the Washington Fault. This fault, trending a little west of north, is hard to see, probably because of its age and the leveling effects of erosion; look for a telltale volcanic cinder cone atop it, approximately north of town, and the position of the sedimentary rocks to the east and west. On the west, about a mile from town, the vermilion Kayenta Formation forms a ledge, which is overlain by the pink Navajo Sandstone. On the east, the multicolored clays of the Chinle Formation may be seen on the upthrown block.

Washington's proximity to St. George has meant that it has now been largely overshadowed by the latter; however, this unassuming town played an important role in the settling of Utah's

Washington's historic cotton mill

Dixie and was one of the first communities to be established here. The settling of Washington was one of the most difficult missions undertaken by the pioneers. The accomplishments of the hardy individuals who toughed out the thankless task are many and have passed into the stuff of local legend.

As early as 1852, one of the original pioneer settlers of the Iron Mission, John D. Lee, thought it feasible to build a community where Washington now stands. His letter to Brigham Young called attention to favorable soil, climate, and excellent possibilities for irrigation. During the next few years, missionaries at Santa Clara Creek successfully raised cotton. As a result, in early 1857, the Church selected a company of 10 families to establish a community here on the Rio Virgin to experiment with the crop. At the April church conference, authorities "called" 28 more families and a few young men, mostly converts from the South, who were thought to be more familiar with cotton production.

The two companies arrived in April and May and began preparing to farm, living in their wagons and dugouts until suitable homes could be built. Mill Creek, and the springs that feed it, provided ample water for household use, with an excess for irrigation. Throughout the years, this small but dependable water supply has been a saving feature of the village. The settlers named

Damming the Rio Virgin

Of all the hardships with which the pioneers in Washington and St. George had to contend, the damming of the Rio Virgin was the most gruelling and certain. This temperamental, turbulent, and exceedingly troublesome stream was a cruel taskmaster. But the people had to dam its waters if they were to fill their irrigation ditches. Faced with the critical problem of inadequate building materials and facilities, they laboriously rolled or dragged brush, rocks, and trees into the channel to build a makeshift dam.

The Virgin River rises on the Markagunt Plateau to the north, and much of this high country is arid, impoverished land, some of it naked rock. With little or no vegetation in the Dixie lowlands to impede the flow, rain from summer thunderstorms rapidly gathers into growing rivulets, later uniting in the tortuous channel of the main stream to produce wild floods of almost unbelievable power. These spasmodic floods tormented Dixie pioneers: dams were often torn out, ditches overflowed or were washed out, and farmlands were left parched and baking in the summer sun. Often these destructive deluges came several times in a single season, and each time they deepened the stream channel, forcing the farmers to bring the brush, rocks, and trees from a greater distance. Nor did time alleviate the problem. On the contrary, the growing herds of livestock grazing the ranges at the Virgin's headwaters increasingly denuded the precious watershed, causing erosion, and adding to the power of the floods.

Although the idea of the spillway—a device whereby a part of the dam is built lower than the rest in order to get rid of excess waters—was developed centuries ago by the Egyptians, it appears that pioneer Dixie farmers conceived of the notion independently. This method helped to contain small floods, but there appeared to be no answer to the big ones.

By 1885 a permanent dam had become a necessity. The men surveyed an appropriate site and decided to construct a pile dam of huge pine logs. A metalurgist at

Enoch, near Cedar City, cast a pile driver and the men hauled logs from the Pine Valley Mountain. Once the piles were deeply driven and the interstices filled with rock, the workers laced the entire structure together to produce one solid unit. On December 7, 1889, just as they were completing the dam, disaster struck. The worst flood ever witnessed in the Rio Virgin promptly reduced their carefully planned dam to a chaotic mass. While the men were in a meeting called to formulate a plan for repair, a second flood completed the destruction.

Someone once said, "There are two kinds of people who stayed in Dixie: those who were too poor to leave, and those who had the courage to battle till the end." Perhaps the group who decided to continue fighting the Rio Virgin was made up of both kinds, but the latter were predominant. A committee was immediately apppointed to locate a new damsite.

Some of the men had noted a place on the Virgin Anticline a few miles up the river where the stream had carved a wide channel through a hogback of resistant Shinarump Conglomerate rock. On the downstream side the channel was quite deep, but the people felt that the tough conglomerate would provide a natural dam. The only problem was that the deep channel needed to be filled in order to push the river upstream far enough to raise the water to the desired level. A survey revealed that a substantial dike, about 600 feet long, would accomplish this purpose.

Once again the Dixie pioneers went to work, and this time fortune smiled. In the winter of 1890, a group of Irish railroad workers who had been snowed in while laboring in the desert to the north, helped with construction. As these men disliked idleness they agreed to work on the dam for their board and to receive "ditch credit" in lieu of wages— a system where the holder is entitled to a share of the irrigation water (a largely valueless commodity to transients).

For several months the men contributed their labor, their machinery, and their skill. After first constructing a

heavy rock core, they slowly dragged masses of earth over the structure and faced it with rock. They completed the dam in 1891, but when the inevitable flood struck, the residents watched heartsick as the dry earth absorbed water and sank. Fortunately, this time help came soon enough to fill the developing holes, and the structure held.

After more than 60 years of struggle and sacrifice, the settlers had tamed the Rio Virgin. But they had paid a price: the population of Washington had been halved by 1892. Shortly after finishing the dam, the residents also completed a 10-mile-long canal. Despite trouble with the soluble gypsum encountered in many places, those persistent farmers were finally able to begin irrigating their fields with a dependable water supply for the entire growing season.

In time, the people of Washington also devised an ingenious way to clear the silt-laden waters of the Rio Virgin. They installed a series of unique sand traps along the ditch, consisting of headgates that opened a few feet below the canal's bottom. The slow-moving water allows the silt to drop to the canal bottom. When sufficient sediment has accumulated the watermaster raises the gates, and some of the water rushes out of the bottom of the canal, carrying the sand from the canal's elevated level back to the river whence it came. While these measures did not improve the quality of the Virgin water for drinking (it was popularly referred to as Virgin Bloat), nevertheless, the people of Washington were now able to modify the river's character sufficiently to provide a reliable water source for irrigation.

their town Washington in honor of the father of their country.

During the first winter there, the outpost was strengthened by the arrival of about 50 Mormon families from San Bernardino, California, who had been recalled to Utah as a confrontation between Johnston's Army and Utah's Mormon population appeared imminent. The following spring all except one of these families moved on.

During the first few years, even the most skilled farmers found it hard to produce good crops in this new land where there was scant information about how to improve the alkaline soil, how to keep crops alive in sizzling desert temperatures, and how to gauge growing seasons. And even when a farmer was able to bring a crop to maturity, he was in constant danger of losing the yield to swarms of hungry grasshoppers. In addition, few settlers understood irrigation. Early on, many people became weakened by malaria, or "ague," a result of the town's proximity to swamps harboring the Anopheles mosquito. Improved drainage later brought the problem under control, but malaria had a devastating effect on the pioneers.

In 1859 Washington became the seat of Washington County. The following season, nurserymen introduced fruit trees and grape vines. By that time, a corn cracker and a grist mill had been built along Mill Creek, where the stream current powered both. Considerable progress in cultivating the sensitive cotton plant had been made, and excellent molasses made from sorghum cane was being used for preserving fruit. These successes notwithstanding, the constant battle with the heat, the malaria, and the river had nevertheless caused many settlers to give up, and by fall 1861 only 20 families remained. The establishing of the Cotton Mission that winter came not a moment too soon; reinforcements

arrived just as the spirits of the Washingtonians had sunk to an all-time low.

In contrast to many Dixie communities, the floods brought on by the Great Rain that winter were probably an asset to Washington: flooding cut the streambeds low enough to drain the swamps and to provide relief from malaria. Brigham Young provided further encouragement in 1865 by planning the construction of a cotton factory in Washington. Using machinery hauled for 1,300 miles by wagon across the plains from the East, the large, rock-walled factory began operations in 1867.

Initially, the manufacture of cotton at the factory proved unprofitable. Feeling that local ownership would provide a needed stimulus, Brigham Young sold his personal interest in the mill to a local cooperative for $44,000, payable in installments. When about $4,000 had been paid, at an obvious hardship, he gave another boost to the enterprise by forgiving the debt. This factory served Dixie well for many years, not only as a source of clothing and employment but also as a general trading post. The "factory script," used to pay workers and to pay for raw materials, quickly became a local medium of exchange. The establishment operated with varying degrees of success until 1910, employing, for a number of years, up to 70 people. Today, visitors may tour the renovated three-story stone building.

The taming of the Rio Virgin in 1892 (see accompanying sidebar) enabled Washington to grow into a prosperous agricultural community, along with some of the population also raising turkeys. Nowadays, the town's proximity to St. George has made it an alternative rest stop for tourists. The addition of Green Springs Golf Course is bringing a new dimension to the economy of the town.

ZION NATIONAL PARK

Elevation: 3,650 to 8,700 feet; population: NPS staff only.

The Paiute Indians called Zion Canyon *i-oo-gune*, meaning "like an arrow quiver." Some early settlers of the region maintained that the Paiute had a superstitious fear of the canyon, but Paiutes today refute that idea, and there is also reliable evidence that they raised corn here. Before the Paiutes, the Anasazi people had used the canyon. Several sites have been found within Zion Canyon, and the remnants of an ancient trail onto the rim are discernible in the vicinity of Weeping Rock.

The first white man to visit Zion seems to have been the Mormon missionary Nephi Johnson, who was "called" to the area in 1858 to locate new sites to be settled. In the winter of 1861–1862 Joseph Black investigated farming possibilities in the canyon. Although he never farmed here, Black built a home in Springdale and gave such glowing accounts of Zion's scenic wonders that the canyon became known as "Joseph's Glory."

Isaac Behunin was the first Anglo to use the canyon, building a summer cabin near the site of today's Zion Lodge in 1863. Behunin named the protected spot "Little Zion," which, although it has several meanings, to the Mormons indicated a place of rest, of security—a place where they could worship their God in peace. Many used the

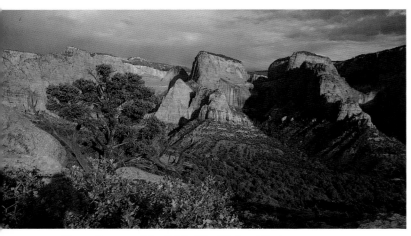

Finger Canyons of the Kolob, Zion National Park

word synonymously with Deseret (Brigham Young's name for the Utah Territory) but to Behunin this canyon was a special haven. He called it "Little Zion," for here the great temples of stone towered above his farm on all sides.

On one of his journeys to the "up river towns," Brigham Young visited the canyon. Some accounts say the road was too rough to permit him to enjoy the scenery; others explain that he was told that some of the inhabitants cultivated tobacco. Regardless of the provocation, he decided the place was "Not Zion," and for years some of his more faithful adherents called it just that.

Behunin was joined shortly by John Rolfe, who built separate dwellings for his two wives in the immediate vicinity; another arrival, William Heap, settled across the Virgin in the mouth of Emerald Pool Canyon. Like other Virgin River Valley families, the residents of Zion moved to Rockville to protect themselves during the Blackhawk War of 1866–1867; however, the men kept up their lands and returned to them with their families as soon as the conflict was resolved.

In 1872, Isaac Behunin sold his holding and moved elsewhere. That same year Major John Wesley Powell, who was headquartered at Kanab, visited Shunesburg and Zion Canyon. The Paiute Indians he encountered at the canyon gave him a name, which he recorded as *mukuntuweap*, meaning "straight canyon." However, William R. Palmer, a Mormon authority on the Paiute Indians, felt that the spelling should be *makun-o-weap* to be so interpreted. The following season Jack Hillers, one of Powell's photographers, took photographs of the area.

The United Order, the experiment by the Mormon Church in cooperative living, was organized in Little Zion in 1874, but lasted only a few months here. When it failed, the remaining colonizers, faced with floods, lack of feed for their animals, and other serious consequences of overgrazing, deserted their farms and moved away. Aside from the meager farming conducted by Springdale residents, little transpired in Little Zion for more than a decade. The notable exception was the visit of Captain Clarence E. Dutton, also of Powell's party, in 1880. During his visit, Dutton penned a matchless description of the sheer-walled canyon in his book, *A Tertiary History of the Grand Canyon District*. His laudatory words focused attention on Zion and had a favorable effect on public opinion.

During one of his early visits to the region, Brigham Young predicted that thousands of feet of lumber would some day come down Zion Canyon. Although good saw timber was abundant on the rims, in the lower, easily accessible areas it was a rare item. Several of Young's followers therefore thought their leader's prediction unlikely to be fulfilled. Nevertheless, as usual, a way was found to make Young's vision a reality. In 1888, during a visit to the East Rim of Zion, David Flanigan came upon rich, mature stands of ponderosa pine. As he gazed into the canyon, he remembered the system of pulleys and wires he had seen used by residents of Shunesburg to convey the mail to the top of the cliffs. He reasoned that if small wires could raise and lower a mail pouch, larger wires, similarly arranged, could carry lumber.

Unable to interest backers in his scheme, Flanigan and his brothers went to the canyon rim in 1900, carrying 50,000 feet of wire with which to perfect the invention. Atop Cable Mountain (a great monolith rising 2,136 feet above the Weeping Rock parking area) Flanigan built a substantial wooden tower and, after much experimentation, evolved a five-wire system that he thought would do the job. In 1904, he purchased a saw mill for operation on the plateau, and, within a short time, Brigham Young's prediction did become a reality.

The original wire was soon replaced by a cable, and some adventurous souls used the device as an elevator to carry them up and down the precipitous walls. Operating successfully for nearly two decades, the cable carried the bulk of the lumber used in the early stages of building Zion Lodge. Unfortunately the system also saw its share of tragedies, and finally one of these resulted in the removal of the cable and the framework at its base. The upper tower was left untouched, however, and can still be seen atop Cable Mountain northeast of the Great White Throne. The story of Flanigan and his cable is told in *An Outstanding Wonder*, available at the visitor center.

Nine geological formations representing the earth's past may be seen in Zion National Park. The oldest stratum visible here is the Kaibab Formation, the rimrock of the Grand Canyon, which may be seen in the northwest corner of the park. This stratum is overlain by the sloping Moenkopi Formation, which is, in turn, succeeded by the distinctive red rocks of the Vermilion Cliffs, consisting of the Chinle (and its member Shinarump Conglomerate), Moenave (and its member Springdale Sandstone), and Kayenta formations. These formations were laid down in a basin fed by streams in which early dinosaurs and other reptiles once lived.

Immediately above them are the precipitous ledges of red to white Navajo Sandstone for which Zion is famous. They were deposited during a time of increasing aridity, when prodigious quantities of wind-blown sand were deposited into great dunes, creating an ancient desert not unlike today's Sahara. These origins are evident in the many swirls found within the formation. Following this period of desertification, streams once more briefly coursed over the desert, sculpting the dunes and laying down clay and silt. Renewed desert conditions occurred for a short time, giving rise to the Temple Cap Formation seen atop the East Temple and West Temple and several other locations. On other "temples," or eroded buttes, the caprock is the resistant, blue-grey Carmel limestone, a formation embedded with sea shells and other fossils. This rock formed when a sea subsequently encroached upon the desert when the climate once more grew moist and cool. The Dakota Formation, made up of conglomerate and fossiliferous sandstone, makes a brief appearance

Bridge Mountain, Zion National Park

on Horse Ranch Mountain, but is confined to this small area of the park. The aggregate thickness of these strata is roughly a mile, with the Navajo Sandstone more than 2,000 feet thick in places.

Hard though it is to imagine, Zion Canyon is largely the work of the tiny Virgin River, which incised a path through the sedimentary rock, exposing the earth's past to scrutiny. Not only are the Rio Virgin and its tributaries responsible for cutting most of the canyon, but their erosive power also removed thousands of tons of sediment from the surrounding rocks. This sediment was whisked away downstream to the rivers' confluences with the Colorado River, and thence to the Gulf of California. Farther upriver, erosion has not yet had time to tear away the younger rocks that complete southern Utah geology. The persistent river continues to attack these strata, though, its sandy waters scouring a relentless path to the sea. As a consequence, Zion Canyon moves slowly northward as the "eternal hills" are worn away.

The snows and rains that fall on the porous sandstone surface play an important part in the destruction of the canyon walls. As rainfall mixes with the air and percolates down through the sandstone, the resulting chemical reaction dissolves the lime cementing the grains together and carries them away. The action of water is most evident at the base of the sandstone, or wherever layers of shale or other impervious beds are found. The more resistant stratum below allows the lime above it to be removed faster here than elsewhere,

leaving behind alcoves in the rock. These alcoves grow larger until eventually they form arches, although the deepening process is often interrupted by vertical cracks and joints in the canyon walls. The arches undermine the cliffs at their base, and, because they are formed by spalling of the rock, are responsible for the canyon's straight walls. Continued erosion eventually weakens the arch, and it falls to the ground. The Great Zion Arch in Zion Canyon is a "blind" arch (meaning that one cannot see daylight through it yet). With persistent weathering, however, a true arch will form at some time in the future, altering the appearance of the cliff wall and eventually leading to its collapse.

In Zion Canyon, the black "desert varnish" that coats the vertical walls as a result of weathering often makes a true interpretation of their structure and composition difficult. But between the Zion Tunnel and the East Entrance to the park where the road winds among the tops of the prehistoric sand dunes, the old sand lines are so acutely defined that their wind-blown nature is unmistakable. At Checkerboard Mesa, horizontally crossbedded, dune-formed rock has been subjected to subsequent vertical jointing, forming a distinctive crisscross pattern that has led to its apt name.

As the plateau rose and broke into blocks along the principal lines of faulting, small faults and breaks developed parallel to the greater fractures. Almost at right angles to the highway, and to Pine Creek, a number of these breaks or joints have been widened by the Pine Creek tributaries. Plants have taken advantage of loose soil in the breaks to gain a foothold in a hostile rock environment.

Zion first came under federal control in 1909 when it was set aside as Mukuntuweap National Monument by presidential proclamation.

In order to photograph all of the easily accessible parts of Zion Canyon, a full day is necessary, or an evening and a morning of good photographic weather. To shoot the scenic regions available by trail, much more time will be required.

The best morning photographs need to be shot before 10:30 and afternoon shots after 2:30, but there are a few places suitable only at or near noon. As a rule, most peaks on the west side of the canyon make good photos in the morning, while those on the east wall are good afternoon subjects.

The following suggestions are based on personal experience and are by no means all-inclusive. Where good "frames" are available they are noted. A park ranger can provide information on photographing seasonal material.

MORNING PHOTOGRAPHS

The West Temple, Three Marys, and associated peaks from either of the two parking areas three miles south of the park boundary—The top of the West Temple, Zion's highest peak, is 7,795 feet above sea level and 4,015 feet above the parking area.

Eagle Crag Peaks—To the south from the same area. These peaks can be recognized from their name.

The Watchman—From the vicinity of the Nature Center. Trees on the lawn to the south provide an excellent frame.

The West Temple, the Towers of the Virgin, and the Altar of Sacrifice—From the visitor center.

The Sentinel—A beautiful view be obtained from the end of the paved path leaving the Court of the Patriarchs parking area.

The Three Patriarchs—A wide angle lens is need to get them all. Otherwise good individual photos of the three may be obtained by climbing to the end of the short trail that winds up the hill from the eastern edge of the parking area.

Cathedral Mountain and Mount Majestic—The tips of these two peaks and the massive red ledges in front of them provide good subject matter when viewed through the trees from a spot about midway down the straight stretch of road south of Zion Lodge.

Castle Dome—The best pictures may be had in the vicinity of the up-canyon approach road to Zion Lodge.

Lady Mountain—This makes an impressive photograph from the Grotto Picnic Area or near vicinity.

The Sentinel and its landslide—This is well captured from the first turn south of the tunnel. As this turn is sharp it's important to park above or below the turn and walk back about a hundred yards. Watch for passing cars.

The Canyon Overlook—This mile-long round-trip hike will provide a splendid view down into the canyon and unsurpassed photographs of the famed Zion switchbacks and some of the tunnel windows.

Wedge Fault—Geologists will find this view interesting. It may be found 0.8 miles east of the end of the big tunnel and 0.6 miles west of the small tunnel. The fault is on the north side of the road.

Normal Fault—Another shot for geologists. This fault is two miles west of the East Entrance checking station and 2.1 miles west of the small tunnel. The road on the east side of the fault provides the best position for a photo and is wide enough to permit parking.

Checkerboard Mesa—Best photographed from a spot about 0.4 miles west of the East Entrance checking station. Use the small parking area just southwest of the concrete bridge. Although there are many other examples of wind deposition and jointing along the road between Checkerboard Mesa and the big tunnel, at no other place are the two shown so well together.

East Entrance—From just outside the park entrance. The sign in the foreground and the peaks beyond provide a good photographic introduction to Zion National Park.

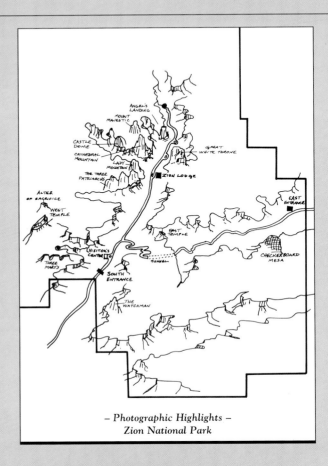

– Photographic Highlights –
Zion National Park

AFTERNOON PHOTOGRAPHS

Angel's Landing—Shoot as early as 2:00 P.M. and before 3:00 P.M. with good results from the vicinity of the Grotto Picnic Area. Good open shots may be obtained from near the river. The light fades on it after 3:30 P.M.

The Great White Throne—An excellent photograph of the "throne" from base to tip may be taken from just east of the first parking area beyond the Weeping Rock. The other classic photo of this symmetrical monolith is made by wading the Rio Virgin above the upper parking area and climbing high onto the opposite hillside. During the summer, watch for rattlesnakes. The foreground from this point begins to "black out" after 2:30 P.M.

Cable Mountain—A good view of this historic mountain may be had from a point between the two Great White Throne parking areas.

Mountain of Mystery—From the end of the Gateway to the Narrows Trail. In late afternoon the foreground may be in heavy shadow.

Red Arch Mountain—This recently formed arch may be shot from the vicinity of the Grotto Picnic Area.

Mountain of the Sun—Capture this formation from the straight stretch of road south of Zion Lodge. The tall trees on either side of the highway will provide a frame.

Mount Spry, the Twin Brothers, the Mountain of the Sun, and Deer Trap Mountain—From the vicinity of the bridge over the Virgin River. An up-canyon shot.

East Temple—Park east of the bridge and walk westward across it for a splendid up-canyon shot. Watch for traffic.

The Watchman—This is the same shot as suggested for the morning. It provides a pleasant contrast with the first.

Bridge Mountain—The trees in the southeast end of the South Campground provide a pleasing frame.

Johnson Mountain—Affords excellent possibilities in the late afternoon from the parking area south of the park.

Eagle Crag Peaks—Same as suggested for the morning. This shot can be taken after most parts of Zion are in deep shadows.

Although Powell's name for the place was not popular, the canyon became increasingly so, and visitors sang its praises to anyone who would listen. As a consequence, the monument was enlarged in 1918 and the name changed to Zion National Monument. The following year Congress set it aside as Zion National Park.

The park was dedicated in 1920, and by 1923, the Utah Parks Company had been organized to operate concessions in the park; (the current concessionaire is TW Services). That same year, the National Park Service constructed revetments to contain the Rio Virgin which, having been released by erosion of overgrazed land, was doing considerable damage. The park service also began to investigate the most feasible route for a highway to connect Zion with Bryce Canyon and Grand Canyon national parks.

The East and West Rim trails were constructed by the park service between 1924 and 1926, at a cost of just under $41,000, a sum appropriated by Congress. In 1925, construction began on the Hidden Canyon and popular Virgin Narrows trails. Engineers had now reached a decision as to the best route for the road that would connect Highway 89 with Highway 9, and contractors excavated the Zion–Mt. Carmel Tunnel between 1927 and 1930. By 1930 this 1.1-mile-long structure and connecting roads had been completed, providing visitors with excellent paved highways to the four national park areas in the vicinity of Zion (Cedar Breaks became a national monument in 1933).

Excepting during World War Two, the increase in travel through Zion has been steady. Today, approximately 2.5 million visitors come to Zion each year. Motoring and bicycling along the paved roads are popular ways to see the national park, but the best way to become really familiar with it is to hike in the narrow side canyons or up to one of Zion's famous rock "temples" on any of the many trails. Stop at the visitor center, located just inside the south entrance of the park, to learn how to make the best use of time in the park.

The wonderfully sculpted Kolob Canyons, established as a national monument by presidential proclamation in 1937, became part of Zion National Park in 1956. Reached via Interstate 15, two miles south of the New Harmony interchange, a paved road 5.2 miles long leads to a section of Zion National Park quite different from Zion Canyon but no less spectacular. This line of cliffs, paralleling Interstate 15, has two great distinctions, topographically speaking. It is the western edge of the Markagunt Plateau and also the western extremity of the Colorado Plateau province, bordering on the Great Basin province that sweeps westwards from here.

The sheer rocks of the Finger Canyons of the Kolob owe their formation to two major geological events. First, a great anticline, or upward folding, was formed, known as the Kanarra Fold. Millions of years later, the Hurricane Fault split along its axis as forces below the earth's surface lifted the eastern section thousands of feet higher than the western section. Subsequent erosion by streams, as well as the combined action of wind and freezing temperatures has sculpted the predominantly red Navajo Sandstone into what may be seen today. In several places, lava flows add a dramatic touch.

Rangers at the visitor center, just off Interstate 15, provide information on the Kolob unit and can suggest ways of seeing the canyons. Hiking into the backcountry here usually requires adequate time and preparation, as distances are great; however, the middle fork of Taylor Creek makes an excellent day hike.

Visitor Services

LOCATION	MOTELS/HOTELS/ CONDOS	FAST FOOD/ RESTAURANTS	RV/TENT CAMPGROUNDS	GAS STATIONS
Alton	–	–	–	–
Anasazi S. P.	–	–	1	–
Asay	–	–	–	–
Beaver	14	10	4	9
Bicknell	2	2	-	-
Boulder	1	2	1	2
Brian Head	2	9	–	–
Bryce Canyon N. P.	4	8	9	5
Calf Creek R. A.	–	–	1	–
Cannonville	–	–	1	–
Capitol Reef N. P.	–	–	1	–
Cedar Breaks N. M.	–	–	1	–
Cedar City	20	28	2	30
Central	–	–	–	–
Circleville	2	1	-	2
Colorado City, AZ	–	1	–	1
Coral Pink Sand Dunes S. P.	–	–	2	–
Duck Creek	4	2	1	2
Duncan's Retreat	–	–	–	–
Enoch	–	–	–	–
Enterprise	–	2	2	2
Escalante & vicinity	4	3	5	3
Fredonia, AZ	2	2	3	4
Georgetown	–	–	–	–
Glen Canyon NRA	5	3+	5, plus shores of Lake Powell	in Page
Glendale	1	1	1	1
Grafton	–	–	–	–
Gunlock S. P.	–	–	1	–
Hamiltons Fort	–	–	–	–
Harrisburg	–	1	1	–
Hatch	4	5	2	4
Henrieville	–	–	–	–
Hildale	–	–	–	–
Hillsdale	–	–	–	–
Hurricane	3	9	4	3
Ivins	–	–	–	–
Johnson	–	–	–	–

LOCATION	MOTELS/HOTELS/ CONDOS	FAST FOOD/ RESTAURANTS	RV/TENT CAMPGROUNDS	GAS STATIONS
Kanab	17	14	3	13
Kanarraville	–	–	1	1
Kodachrome Basin S. P.	–	–	1	–
La Verkin	–	1	2	2
Leeds	1	–	1	1
Loa	3	1	-	-
Milford	1	1	-	2
Moccasin, AZ	–	1	1	–
Mt. Carmel	3	2	3	2
Navajo Lake	–	–	2	–
New Clifton	–	–	–	–
New Harmony	–	–	–	–
Orderville	3	2	1	4
Page, AZ	5	4+	1	9
Panguitch (and Panguitch Lake)	18	10	9	8
Paria	–	–	–	–
Parowan area	6	7	7	6
Pine Valley R. A.	1	1	3	–
Pinto	–	–	–	–
Pintura	–	–	–	–
Pipe Spring N. M., AZ	–	1	1	–
Quail Creek S. P.	–	–	1	–
Rockville	–	–	–	–
St. George	39	67	6	33
Santa Clara	–	–	–	2
Shunesburg	–	–	–	–
Silver Reef	–	–	–	–
Snow Canyon S. P.	–	–	1	–
Springdale	15	10	1	3
Summit	–	–	–	1
Torrey	4	2	1	3
Toquerville	1	–	–	–
Tropic	3	1	2	3
Veyo	–	2	1	2
Virgin City	1	1	1	–
Washington	1	3	1	5
Zion N. P.	1	2	1	–

For further information, please consult:

Utah Travel Council
publishers of
Utah Scenic Byways and Backways
Council Hall / Capitol Hill
Salt Lake City, UT 84114
(801) 538-1030

Color Country Travel Region
237 North Bluff, Suite #2
St. George, UT 84770
(801) 628-4171

Utah State Parks, Southwest Region
P.O. Box 1079
Cedar City, UT 84720-1079
(801) 586-4497

Dixie National Forest
82 North 100 East
Cedar City, UT 84720
(801) 865-3700

BLM Utah State Office
324 South State Street
Salt Lake City, UT 84145-0155
(801) 539-4021

BLM Cedar City District Office
176 East D.L. Sargent Drive
Cedar City, UT 84720
(801) 586-2401

Utah Department of Transportation
4501 South 2700 West
Salt Lake City, UT 84119
(801) 965-4000

Bryce Canyon National Park
Bryce Canyon, UT 84717
(801) 834-5322

Capitol Reef National Park
Torrey, UT 84775
(801) 425-3791

Zion National Park
Springdale, UT 84767
(801) 772-3256

Cedar Breaks National Monument
Cedar City, UT 84720
(801) 586-9451

Glen Canyon National Recreation Area (Lake Powell)
337 North Navajo, Page, AZ 86040
(602) 645-2471